Gerald R. Ford

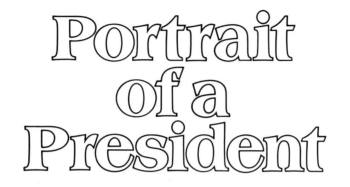

Portrait of a President

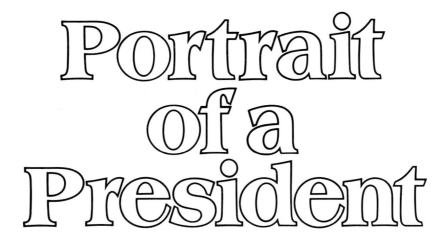

Portrait of a President

Text/Hugh Sidey·Photographs/Fred Ward

Harper & Row, Publishers

New York   Evanston   San Francisco   London

For my wife, Charlotte—F. W.

For my father and mother, Kenneth and Alice Sidey—H. S.

PRESIDENTIAL PORTRAIT. Text copyright © 1975 by Hugh Sidey. Photographs © 1975 by Fred Ward. All rights reserved. Printed in the United States of America. No part of this book may be used or reproduced in any manner whatsoever without written permission except in the case of brief quotations embodied in critical articles and reviews. For information address Harper & Row, Publishers, Inc., 10 East 53rd Street, New York, N.Y. 10022. Published simultaneously in Canada by Fitzhenry & Whiteside Limited, Toronto.

75 76 77 78 79 10 9 8 7 6 5 4 3 2 1

Four pictures in this book, those on pages 14, 15, 136 and 169, are of events that took place in the period before Fred Ward had begun work on this book. These were taken by David Hume Kennerly and are properly credited as White House photographs.

Library of Congress Cataloging in Publication Data
Sidey, Hugh.
    Portrait of a president.
    1. Ford, Gerald R., 1913-
    I. Ward, Fred, 1935-   II. Title.
E866.S56   1975   973.925'092'4 [B]
    74-28795
ISBN 0-06-013869-6
FIRST EDITION

Feb 26 75

Design by Bob Nemser   **A BLACK STAR BOOK**

Contents

A NOTE FROM THE PHOTOGRAPHER

To photograph a book of this type requires special arrangements, clearances and cooperation on the part of many people. Foremost, my gratitude and appreciation go to President Ford, who had the openness and trust to believe in the idea and who made the commitment to have me stay near him for the necessary two months. Such faith and cooperation had never before been shown to a photographer who was not in the employ of the government. Not once did the President ask to review my material or limit my access to him. Betty Ford and other members of the family agreed to every photographic request, and I shall always remember their spirit and enthusiasm.

Sincere thanks also go to David Kennerly, the President's personal photographer. Dave immediately saw the value of this book as a historical document and generously gave his time and efforts to assure that the bureaucracy did not stand in the way of the photographs. Without him there would have been no book. His staff aided me in countless ways and has my gratitude. Ricardo Thomas, Karl Schumacher, Sandra Eisert, Bill Fitz-Patrick and Jack Kightlinger were of constant assistance.

Dick Keiser, the Secret Service Special Agent in Charge of the Presidential Protective Division, assured my access to the President when we were outside the White House. Don Rumsfeld, coordinator of operations at the White House, assisted me in my work with the various staff members.

To the senior staff, Ron Nessen and his press office personnel, and the many government officials who cooperated in this work, I express my thanks.

Howard Chapnick of Black Star and Nach Waxman of Harper & Row had sufficient confidence in the book from its inception to work tirelessly toward its successful completion. They were a constant and much appreciated support.

I could never recognize all those who offered advice, encouragement and criticism. To my wife, Charlotte, and to those many other friends, I simply say, I know and I thank you.

F. W.

Technical Data

All the photographs were taken with 35-mm Canon, Leica and Nikon equipment. The Tri-X film was rated at ASA 800 and processed in D-76. All processing and printing were done at G and W Lab at Black Star in New York City.

PREFACE

This is a glimpse. It is a fragment of a
President's life, neither definitive nor
encompassing. It is a brief portrait of
Gerald R. Ford, President through an
accident of history, in his first months
of power. Impressions are drawn but
no lasting observations are offered.
Hints are given of his directions, but no
final conclusions are even sketched. Yet
there are in Presidents, as in all people,
certain enduring characteristics that
are there at birth, defined in childhood
and tempered in adult life. These tell
us much about why they do what they
do, what they may do in the future. It
is our hope that this volume of pictures
and words captures some of those
special dimensions of Gerald Ford and
will help the reader to better understand him as a man and as a President.

Transition

Rarely had the White House been the scene of such a range of emotion as on August 9, when Richard Nixon walked out of the presidency and Gerald Ford took over. From Nixon's rambling and tearful farewell in the East Room, where the audience sat crushed and humiliated by the burden of a disgraced President, to the moment that Ford raised his hand and took the oath was only about two hours. Fred Ward followed the drama through his camera, standing in the East Room as the distraught Nixon tried to explain himself to the troubled members of his fading administration, then following Nixon out to the South Lawn for the final exit. The picture of the Nixons and the Fords walking down the red carpet toward the helicopter that would take the Nixons away from the White House shows the nadir of the emotional morning, in Ward's view. The swiftness of the transference of power amazed Ward. The tragedy of Pat Nixon—her silent but evident suffering—brought waves of sympathy. For the first time the new President and his wife became visible. The Fords stopped halfway down the carpet, bid their final good-bys; the Nixons went to the helicopter's door and within seconds were vanishing beyond the Washington Monument, which stands on the Ellipse below the White House. Hope was born anew. Gerald and Betty Ford walked back into the White House, new lives in the continuing spectacle of the American presidency.

Power does not wait. Within a few days of Nixon's departure from the White House, the trappings of the presidency reflected the presence of Gerald Ford. The traces of Nixon had been excised, the apparatus of authority given the signature of the new man. Fred Ward had gone to the Cabinet Room to wait for Ford's arrival at a meeting with his economic advisers. The photographer walked quietly around the room, came to the back of the President's massive black leather chair, which stands at the center of the elliptical table. He was struck again by the suddenness of change. The brass nameplate with the date of Ford's in-auguration seemed fixed and comfortable, as if it had been there for weeks or years. Fred bent down so the light would be just right on the engraved name, otherwise the nameplate would just catch a glare from the tall windows that open east on the Rose Garden. The hexagonal spots behind are the images of the light bulbs in the wall fixtures. They take on the shape of the camera lens diaphragm when they are so far out of focus. The President seemed at home by this time, September 1974. He strode in, shook the hands of a few men near him, went straight to his chair and pulled it out, then settled into another of the countless meetings that go on in the Cabinet Room, the place where much of the federal government's policy is planned. This was the beginning of daily meetings with economic experts, labor leaders and industrialists to plan Ford's first efforts to halt inflation and stem the economic recession.

THE
PRESIDENT
AUGUST 9, 1974

Gerald R. Ford did not know the precise moment he became the thirty-eighth President of the United States. Only two men did. Secretary of State Henry Kissinger, on the morning of August 9, 1974, was alone in his office in the West Wing of the White House, waiting for General Alexander Haig, the chief of Richard Nixon's staff. Standing beside the round table in the corner of his office, he was looking out the tall window up the northwest drive. Television broadcasters and technicians scurried back and forth across the lawn, setting up their positions so the cameras would frame the stately columns of the north portico as a backdrop. Beyond the high iron fence clusters of people stood in silence and wonder, peering into the White House grounds for some glimpse of the powerful and the famous.

Kissinger, the most remarkable and successful of all the men who had come to Washington with Richard Nixon, had watched other political spectacles from that same window—the Vietnam war protest marches that filled Pennsylvania Avenue; the jubilant inaugural parade following Nixon's smashing 1972 electoral victory. But there had been nothing like this in his time, or for that matter in all of American history. The most powerful man in the world stood convicted by public opinion of "high crimes and misdemeanors" against his own nation and against the office with which he was entrusted. He was resigning.

The final moment had arrived. The night before, Nixon had told the nation of his intentions. He had bid good-by to his cabinet and staff in a rambling, tearful epilogue to twenty-eight years of politics. Now he was airborne, on his way back to California. The gleaming Air Force One was high over the flat corn land of central Missouri.

It was a few moments after eleven-thirty, and by prearrangement Haig was stepping down the carpeted back corridor of the White House. The Secretary of State is the official of the United States government who must accept and certify resignations. Haig carried eight copies of the letter. It was one sentence long. A sentence of shattering import. "Dear Mr. Secretary: I hereby resign the Office of President of the United States. Sincerely, Richard Nixon." Haig entered Kissinger's office silently. The Secretary took the letters from the presidential aide and sat down at the round table. "They all have to be initialed and the time noted," said Haig. It was 11:35 a.m. There was silence again as Kissinger quickly, firmly scribbled his "11.35 A M HK " Gerald Ford had become President in this minuscule, arcane ritual of deliverance. Haig scooped up the papers and walked back down the hall to prepare for the swearing-in ceremony at noon. Enveloped in a profound sadness, Kissinger began to gear himself for the future. He had been living through some of the most painful hours of his life but now there was hope the nightmare was fading.

Across the street from the White House, on the second floor of the old, gray Executive Office Building, Ford was making last-minute preparations before walking over to the East Room to take his oath. Those who saw him in these minutes after the presidential mantle had settled on his shoulders found him to be a confident and comfortable man. He was immersed in the details of his speech, of the actions that would give America its first taste of the new President, a man who had not been elected to the office by the people. There was in the dim halls of the EOB and about the White House itself the emotional eddy that always accompanies the transfer of presidential power, whether by death or, as in this case, by constitutional process. It is grief mixed with exhilaration, it is fear overlaid

with courage. It is hesitation washed away by the smell of new adventure.

I had watched this singular human drama in front of an ugly brick hospital in Dallas on November 22, 1963. The murder of John Kennedy had brought as much shock to Lyndon Johnson and his aides as to the others traveling in the presidential party on that sunny political outing. But the realization that they at last had the power they had vainly sought for so long was too heady to subdue even in those anguished hours. The Johnson men collided in the use of their authority with the shattered men and women who had come to Dallas with Kennedy. They fought their own impulses, pitting compassion and their sense of what was appropriate against what they perceived as their duty in a time of national crisis.

Some of the same peculiar aura hangs over even a scheduled inauguration of a new President where there are in attendance an election winner and a loser. I had watched Richard Nixon come down off the inaugural stand after John Kennedy became President on a cold, bright day in 1961. Nixon's eyes were sad, his hands jammed in his overcoat pockets, an ex-Vice-President, a vanquished presidential candidate. He had moved quickly to his limousine, slipped into it almost unnoticed and left Washington believing he would not return.

On August 9 as noon approached, the newborn Ford administration was caught in this same tension of somber hope. Ford had carefully selected some 250 guests for the historic occasion. They were gathering in the East Room, many of them still red-eyed from their weeping, stunned from having seen Richard Nixon two hours earlier saying good-by in disgrace and despair. But there was a fresh feeling too, the tingle of a new beginning. Nixon's White House had been a fortress of despondency in those last days. Suspicion and hate had lifted insurmountable barriers to all

but a few who dwelled in the outside world. Now sunlight was beginning to filter in again. The entire Michigan congressional delegation had been invited, among them people like Senator Robert Griffin, who had helped force Nixon out of power. Ford's limousine driver and the family maid had been included and so had all eleven of the incumbent congressmen who were first elected with Ford in 1948.

Former New York Senator Charles Goodell, a liberal Republican and Ford friend whom Nixon and his political hatchet man Spiro Agnew had deliberately scuttled in 1972, was back in the White House for the first time in years. There were some who remembered that election vignette of Agnew gloating before the TV screen when Goodell's defeat was confirmed. "We got that son of a bitch," muttered Agnew then. The bearded liberal Democratic senator from Michigan, Phil Hart, took his place quietly on a gilt chair. Also there was Don Riegle, Jr., a Michigan congressman who had deserted the Republicans and become a Democrat in 1973 when he saw the way Nixon was leading the Grand Old Party. All were welcome. Ford was pulling on the strings of government, gathering them all under one roof in a ritual of healing. The cabinet was there and the Joint Chiefs of Staff with their chests full of medals, led by their chairman, General George Brown. The men from the agencies took their seats, and the leaders from Congress. Behind them the reporters from the White House press corps stood and watched, pencils and pads ready. The TV cameras winked back and forth and the still cameramen crouched and bent as they caught the approach of men of importance. The East Room was radiant, its parquet floors polished to a mirror

finish, its windows sparkling, the historic eight-foot-high oil portraits of George and Martha Washington presiding over the whole incredible scene. Yet it was no more spectacular than what some others had witnessed in that room and in that house. (Actually, the East Room itself had a modest inauguration. Before it was finished, Abigail Adams would come down and hang out her wash there to dry.) In August 1814, Dolly Madison cut the canvas of Washington out of its frame when she heard the British were on their way. She rolled it carefully, packed it in her wagon and fled into the Virginia night. The British burned the inside of the White House but they did not stay long. Dolly returned and so did the portrait. Much later, Harry Truman had played the piano in the East Room and Lyndon Johnson had danced on those smooth floors into the small hours of the night, squeezing his partners exuberantly in all the right places.

Not all the people swept up in the events of August 9 that swirled through the White House were people of power or position. Roger Porter, twenty-eight, a Harvard student and former Rhodes scholar, had been accepted earlier in the summer as a White House fellow to work on the staff of Vice-President Ford. The day before, he had been driving down from Cambridge to report for duty when he turned on his car radio. He heard that President Nixon would make his national television address that night and it probably would be a resignation speech. Porter's world was suddenly changed. He hurried on along the turnpikes and arrived at a friend's house in the Washington suburbs just before Nixon came on the air. He sat in silence as he heard the news. He had a job, but now it was to be with a President. Porter walked into the Vice-President's offices at 8:30 a.m. on August 9 and

instantly was in the midst of the transition maelstrom that swept through the EOB that day. L. William Seidman, an accountant from Grand Rapids who had long been a friend and counselor to Ford, took Porter under his wing. The young man was given an empty desk and from there he watched history made. Once, just before noon, he looked down the hall and in that moment he saw Ford stride out of his office and get on the elevator on his way to the East Room. Shortly afterward, perched on the edge of a chair in front of a television set, Porter found himself next to Pennsylvania's former governor William Scranton, a Ford friend called in to help recruit new people for the administration. It had all the elements of a novel, and Porter relished it, sitting riveted as Ford's image came on the screen.

In the East Room just after noon, one of the White House military aides announced, "Ladies and gentlemen, the Chief Justice of the United States." The silver-haired Warren Burger marched in with his black robes on. It was an ironic turn. Burger had been Nixon's choice to head the court, a safe conservative, Nixon had calculated. Yet it had been Burger on the fateful July 24 who had read the Supreme Court opinion ordering Nixon to turn over the Watergate tapes that would bring about his downfall. On that earlier day, out in San Clemente, where Nixon had sealed himself away from the world to await the verdict, there had been unabashed fury. Nixon had stormed and sworn against the jurist from Minnesota, who had never, throughout the weeks of secret deliberation, any second thoughts about his position. It was another manifestation of the curious moral illness of Nixon that right and wrong did not matter. All that mattered was the expediency of power, the obligation of position. Somehow Nixon had led himself to believe that he owned Burger or at least a part of him.

Ford had wanted Burger for this inaugural ceremony and had called

him back from the Netherlands. The Chief Justice had flown off for his first extended vacation since 1969, when he had been named to the court. He was a bicycle buff and had planned to cycle around the Netherlands a bit, then head south for some sun. It was not to be. The White House operators, who, John Kennedy had said, could raise Lazarus, found him in the residence of our ambassador. By that time it was too late for a commercial connection to the States and a military jet was ordered for the flight. The Chief Justice touched down just two hours before the swearing in.

Behind Burger came Gerald and Betty Ford. The people in the East Room were on their feet. They cheered and applauded. The sadness and the despair, the months of bitter memories, seemed to recede in that moment. The Fords stood smiling. Those who watched marveled at how simple it all was. There were no tanks in the streets, there were no disaffected groups locked in bitter contention. The power had passed by constitutional process with a minimum of turmoil. Richard Nixon's jet was fleeing toward the far horizon while the nation turned to the east and that small stage in the White House. "Mr. Vice-President," said Warren Burger, "are you prepared to take the oath of office as President of the United States?" As if he had rehearsed the line for weeks (and he may have), Ford answered, "I am, sir." Strange, these two men were both out of the prairie, men of the middle distances of their vast land. The six-foot Ford topped Burger by half an inch. The Bible that Betty Ford held was opened to the Book of Proverbs, third chapter, fifth and sixth verses. It was the passage which Ford, an Episcopalian, repeated every night as a prayer. "Trust in the Lord with

13

all thine heart; and lean not unto thine own understanding. In all thy ways acknowledge him, and he shall direct thy paths." It was three minutes past noon. Burger's hand was up. Ford's too. Ford's voice was steady, firm, as he repeated the short, simple oath of office, one of those capsules of lofty purpose that have characterized this nation from its beginning. All the meaning was there. It was this same oath that Richard Nixon had violated. "I, Gerald R. Ford, do solemnly swear that I will faithfully execute the office of President of the United States, and will to the best of my ability, preserve, protect and defend the Constitution of the United States, so help me God." There is no higher charge of responsibility. There is no more eloquent statement of dedication. It settled over Gerald Ford. The people in the East Room sensed it, and as the Chief Justice reached to shake Ford's hand they rose to applaud. This was a new beginning. In that moment, Burger searched for some way to express his relief and his joy in the system of government that had brought the orderly change of command. He turned to Hugh Scott, who was applauding nearby. Burger grabbed Scott's hand and, in a rush, said, "Hugh, it worked. Thank God, it worked."

Ford's brief inaugural address beamed out to a waiting nation was assuring. "I am acutely aware that you have not elected me as your President by your ballots," he said. "So I ask you to confirm me as your President with your prayers....I believe that truth is the glue that holds governments together...I expect to follow my instincts of openness and candor...." The weary men of Nixon's reign of deception sat with their wives on the front row of chairs, a hope kindling that now they could devote their full energies to their jobs. William Simon, the Secretary of the

Treasury, clasped his hands on his knees, a slight frown creasing his brow. And Kissinger, who had officiated at Nixon's end, let a smile play across his mouth as Ford talked. "My fellow Americans," declared the new President, "our long national nightmare is over. Our Constitution works. Our great republic is a government of laws and not of men. Here, the people rule.... As we bind up the internal wounds of Watergate, more painful and more poisonous than those of foreign wars, let us restore the Golden Rule to our political process. And let brotherly love purge our hearts of suspicion and of hate...."

It was part sermon, part profession of humility, part prayer of hope. It was much like Ford himself.

Jerry Ford never wanted to be President. "My ambition was to be Speaker of the House someday," he explained on an evening after he had moved into the Oval Office. "But things did not break that way." As minority leader of the House, Ford had resigned himself to retiring before the Democratic majority could be overturned.

When did Ford himself first begin to see the possibility of his becoming President? Even he is not exactly sure. But the men of congressional politics like Ford, who live and work by instinct and the sense of events, get such tremors long before others do. On October 10, 1973, when Spiro Agnew resigned as Vice-President, Melvin Laird, former congressman and former Secretary of Defense, was with Ford. The two had been close friends in the House and had continued the relationship as Laird moved in and out of the Nixon administration. As Laird recalled, he had a feeling deep down somewhere that Ford was about to be touched by fate, although Nixon had given no hint where he might turn for Agnew's successor. "Jerry," said Laird on an impulse, looking directly at his old friend, "someday you are going to be President."

When Ford got the call to be the new Vice-President, the strong possibility that he might in time succeed Nixon was common speculation. Ford knew the growing seriousness of the Watergate crisis. But because he was in a position demanding loyalty to the President, he publicly discouraged talk of moving up, while privately he let his mind explore the dimensions of presidential responsibility. On a campaign trip he talked with reporter John Osborne, of the *New Republic*, about the kind of cabinet he might have if Nixon was forced from office. Though embarrassed by the flap the story caused, Ford did not deny that he had said it all. But he went even deeper behind the vice-presidential veil as he struggled to walk the line between reality and his sense of obligation to Nixon.

Others within the government were not so inhibited. They began to consider Ford in their future. A shadow presidency developed through the early months of 1974. Those cabinet officers whom Ford had named favorably in his musings moved to establish closer contacts with the Vice-President's office. Those who had not been on that list called around Washington to inquire among Ford's friends how they could enhance their standing with the Vice-President. And of course the congressmen facing reelection began to talk openly of how much better their political prospects would be if Ford were in the White House. Even legislation began to get a touch of Ford. At the Department of Health, Education and Welfare, a staff member helping design a new welfare program for the Nixon White House was asked by a colleague if he had considered the Vice-President's position on the issues involved, since Ford might well be the man responsible for passing the bill. So the new staffer dug into the record to learn Ford's congressional voting record and give the new bill a bit of the Ford flavor.

One morning in April, the Chowder and Marching Society, the Republican social and study group to which Ford and Nixon had both belonged in their early congressional years, called in pollster Louis Harris for some political talk. Harris chortled as he confided to a friend afterward that one after another of the worried men, between bites of scrambled eggs, asked if they could not salvage some House seats from the looming election disaster if they forced Nixon out and got Ford into office. Harris was cautiously affirmative, although by then the Watergate erosion was so bad there was some question whether anything would help.

Early in 1974 Henry Kissinger became more diligent in his briefings for the Vice-President. When the Secretary of State negotiated the disengagement in the Middle East, he called Ford, who was in Michigan, and filled him in before the public announcement was made so that Ford could use the event in the day's speeches. Secretary of Defense Schlesinger, who had come in for some mild Ford criticism on his relations with Congress, moved quickly to explain himself and to improve his bedside manner when on the Hill.

Ford moved through the gathering Watergate storm with good humor and considerable skill, upholding his loyalty to the presidency while worrying aloud about the effects of Watergate, proclaiming Nixon's technical innocence based on the evidence available, then refusing to study selected tapes that the President had offered him privately as proof of his lack of guilt.

Peter Rodino's House Judiciary Committee ground out its devastating indictment of Nixon and his aides. They were torturous days for any man of conscience. Ford was not the only Republican guilty of conflicting statements, given to

profound public discouragement one day and then leading the attack against the Nixon foes the next day. Inconsistency in the fluid political world is taken for granted. Ford was responding with the pragmatism that had served him well in his nine years as minority leader, a post in which each day's legislative battles require some new refinement of one's philosophical moorings. A man of Ford's perception could not have clung to the idea that Nixon was innocent. But there was a desperation growing out of Ford's congressional experience which prompted him to erect his elaborate façade while searching privately, although vainly, for some other route of escape for Nixon and for the Republicans.

On the morning of Thursday, August 1, Haig called Ford and asked to come to his office at the EOB. There, Haig told Ford there was new evidence on the tapes that would be delivered to District Judge John Sirica the following Monday. When it emerged publicly, said Haig, it was apt to tip the balance for the impeachment of Nixon in the House, an action which already had been recommended by the Judiciary Committee. Haig called back later that same day and asked for another meeting with Ford as soon as possible. At three-thirty the concerned Haig was again sitting with the Vice-President. He had more details now about the catastrophic nature of the evidence against Nixon. Was Ford prepared to take over the presidency? Haig asked. Jerry Ford said he was.

And yet the drama had to be played out fully. Ford took off on his campaigning as if nothing had happened. In New Orleans he conceded that the situation in the House had eroded and that Nixon might be impeached. Then, as if by reflex, out of fear that he would do something to appear as if he were pushing Nixon out the door, Ford declared that he still felt

Nixon was "innocent of any impeachable offenses." At that time Nixon had gone to Camp David and there had begun his epic struggle with himself. On Monday, August 5, Nixon released the part of the June 23, 1972, tape that showed he had ordered the Watergate cover-up long before he had admitted in his public statements that he knew anything about it. Ford learned of Nixon's action as he flew back from the South in his Convair turboprop. Immediately he sat down and drafted a statement of official neutrality that would protect his credibility for the job that was rushing in on him. "The public interest," Ford announced, was "no longer served" by his continuing to speak out on impeachment.

As Nixon's world began to fall apart, Ford retreated discreetly to his Alexandria, Virginia, home. When the new evidence was made public, the stunned Republican loyalists of the House Judiciary Committee reversed themselves and announced support of the articles of impeachment. But Nixon was not quite ready to give up his fight. On his yacht, *Sequoia*, cruising the Potomac that night, he received a radio phone call from Haig reporting on the reaction. They had lost all their support, Haig said. "Soft bastards," Nixon muttered. With the inevitability of impeachment staring him in the face, his orders were to move his defenses as quickly as possible to the Senate, where the trial would take place. The next morning the cabinet met and Nixon repeated his determination to fight to the end. Ford listened silently, as did the others, which was the difference between that meeting and earlier cabinet meetings. Not one of the men present jumped to Nixon's defense. No one raised the banner of defiance on Nixon's behalf as some had in earlier sessions in which Watergate had been discussed. By that time Haig and Kissinger had assumed the leadership in orchestrating a quiet end to the Nixon tragedy. Both men, perhaps the most influential two remaining on the inner White House team, had, since

The quiet hours. When that last meeting with his aides is completed on a routine day, Ford uses the time before dinner at the residence to catch up on the day's reading, an immense and never-ending duty. It was about 6 p.m. when Fred Ward slipped outside the Oval Office onto the portico that borders the office. He took this picture through the bushes. Ford was at his desk, unmoving, deep in concentration. On this day, September 30, Betty Ford was still in the hospital after her cancer operation, Ford still trying to master the details of his routine. Fred noticed that each time he watched this evening ritual the dark came earlier. But the President did not leave his desk sooner. Toward 7 p.m. he would stir himself and put the unfinished reading matter into a briefcase, which would be sent to the residence for attention after dinner. Then Ford, with an aide or two, would walk outdoors under the portico and on to the White House living quarters.

first learning of the new evidence, known that Nixon would have to leave office. They had counseled cabinet members and Republicans on the Hill to use restraint in their contacts with the President for fear that demands for his resignation would harden his determination and increase his personal tragedy.

Jerry Ford was visible but quiet. He breakfasted with eight young Republican members of the House, who came away feeling that he was ready to assume the presidency. He met with members of the Senate Republican policy group, avoiding any discussion of his role in the week's mounting crisis. He talked with visiting Japanese legislators, conferred with members of the distressed home-building industry. He even granted two long-scheduled interviews with reporters, again talking innocuously of the storm that was raging outside his quiet office. He met with Navy Secretary J. William Middendorf and Admiral James Holloway and they gave him a picture of the U.S.S. *Monterey*, the aircraft carrier on which Ford had served in the Pacific during World War II. As events moved toward a climax, Ford was feeling it more and more. At his home Wednesday night, August 7, he took his usual swim in his heated pool. In one quiet moment he looked wistfully at the inviting water. "I really hate to leave this pool," he said. Jerry Ford was ready.

Yet still the word had not been spoken. Nixon vacillated. He had talked to Kissinger after the cabinet meeting about the possibility of resigning. Kissinger had told the President then that he thought resignation was the best way out. Still, Nixon's family, clinging to any thin straws of innocence that only those so close can perceive in such moments, wanted him to stand the Senate im-peachment trial. On Wednesday night Nixon reached his conclusion and told his family. He called Kissinger in, and for two hours these two men who had been through so much together in the political struggles of the world talked. The distraught Nixon rambled about his life as midnight approached. He told about his family, about his Quakerism, about his belief in prayer. He wanted to know if he would be remembered as a President who had brought peace in a dangerous time. Kissinger assured him he would be. They parted and Kissinger went back to his White House office. The phone rang and it was Nixon again. He wanted to talk some more, a man reaching for a life that he had gloried in but was now ebbing.

On Thursday morning, August 8, Nixon asked Ford to come to the Oval Office. Ford knew that this was likely to be the time when Nixon would tell him of his intention to resign. Still, it was not, even then, absolutely settled. Before Ford went in to see the President, Haig told him that Nixon was having doubts. At some moments he was certain that he had made up his mind to resign, Haig reported. Then Nixon would wonder if he shouldn't fight on. Haig said it was likely Nixon would resign but that Ford should be prepared for almost anything. Ford strode into the office, over the bright blue carpet with the American Eagle woven into the center. Nixon was at his desk, looking down. Nothing was said and Ford took the chair beside the President's desk. For a few seconds Nixon continued to study the papers in front of him. Then he looked up at Ford. "Jerry," he said, "I know you'll do a good job."

The First Days

The center of command, the Oval Office. This picture was taken from behind the President, showing most of the graceful chamber in which Presidents have worked since the time of Theodore Roosevelt, who had the West Wing of the White House constructed. In this afternoon meeting of October 14, Ford is discussing energy matters with Secretary of the Interior Rogers C. B. Morton, right, and Robert Hartmann, principal political adviser and speechwriter in Ford's first weeks. The talk on this afternoon was how to fit energy planning into Ford's developing economic plan. Hartmann was taking notes to include in a speech he was drafting for the President. The brilliant blue oval rug with the gold stars around the border was left from the Nixon period, as were some of the decorations on the walls. They would be changed when Mrs. Ford regained her strength following her hospitalization. Unlike Nixon, who did not spend many hours in the Oval Office, Ford used it extensively in the first months, both for ceremonial affairs and for work. His routine was to stay at his desk when dealing with such familiar figures as Morton and Hartmann, but to move to the couches by the fireplace when he had outside visitors.

The White House and its environs form a city within the larger District of Columbia. It is the heart of the government but it is more. It is a man's office and a family's home. It is a museum, a dazzling repository of American treasures and traditions. It is eighteen manicured acres in the midst of a cemented urban area.

There are Concord grapes there, growing over an arbor built in the Jacqueline Kennedy garden. In summer they hang heavy and inviting, thrilling the ladies who come for tea and are allowed to pluck one or two to eat. Chief Gardener Irvin Williams has a fine box of herbs, ranging from chives to thyme, growing on the roof of the White House, and Henry Haller, the chief White House cook, uses them when he prepares state dinners. Out back, the American elm tree planted by John Quincy Adams presides over more than 5,000 shrubs and trees, its mighty crown eighty feet high and still growing. There are six gardeners from the National Park Service who tend all this vegetation and weed the intricate flower beds Mrs. Paul Mellon had planted in the Rose Garden for John Kennedy.

Milton Pitts, who barbered Richard Nixon's hair, still presides in his basement shop. When Gerald Ford came around for his first trim, the President carefully explained his hair problems to Pitts. His hair, he observed, bulged on the sides, was too thin on the top. "What am I doing wrong?" asked Ford as the genial Pitts surveyed the presidential dome. "Just about everything, Mr. President," said Pitts. "With your hair, that is," he quickly added. Ford roared with laughter and signaled Pitts to give him one of his skilled trims.

Dr. William Lukash has an office on the ground floor of the White House. There is a nurse on duty and, of course, all necessary emergency equipment. When the President travels, Lukash is by his side with his black bag, which may in these times be almost as important as the traveling military secrets.

There is a movie theater in the White House; on demand, the latest films are served up for presidential review. Richard Nixon had a small bowling alley installed in the basement, perhaps to compensate for covering up Franklin Roosevelt's swimming pool with the offices of the White House press corps. Nixon was not a swimmer but Ford is, and that has caused some problems. There is a curator to look after the art objects, antiques and furniture.

One White House worker does nothing but wash windows and chandeliers. When he finishes he starts over again. They do the laundry in the White House basement, bake cakes for the big bashes and turn out the cookies for Christmas. There is a tennis court which President Ford has actually used, and there is a dog kennel to accommodate animals that may come with the tenants or be acquired. The Kennedys let Caroline's pony, Macaroni, graze on the blue grass and pull a tiny sleigh over the snow one winter, the scene ending up on the presidential Christmas card for that year.

A President can get massages on request. His tailors come to him when he wants suits, and his valet shines his shoes. Priceless art from the national collection can be borrowed for the White House walls. Party invitations are inscribed by some of the most skillful calligraphers in the country.

When the President and his family travel, the helicopters settle on the South Lawn just a few yards from the rear entrance. A Navy air control officer hides under the big leaves of one of the two magnolias planted by Andrew Jackson. Without touching a suitcase or worrying about the time, the President can stroll to his waiting chopper, buckle in and be lifted over the lawn to Andrews Air Force Base. As he rides he can have a drink if he chooses and look at the fine prints that are mounted on the helicopter's paneled walls. At Andrews he is gently deposited some twenty-five yards from his big jet. The moment he sits down the plane starts to roll. Under normal conditions it takes him about three and a half minutes to get to the head of the runway and twenty-two seconds to lift off the ground. All calculated with precision, it does not dare fail and has not. Aloft, the President can watch color television, converse by phone with any place on the globe, read the latest intelligence cables clacking in over the special communications gear. He has a bed, a lounge, two kitchens and three lavatories, and everybody else flying that day has to get out of his aircraft's way.

There are 3,000 people who make this presidential life style possible on that small federal island. Another 300,000 members of the executive structure are scattered in nearby buildings, and of course the President can call on the services of thousands more around the nation, all in the administration.

It was this incredible apparatus that Gerald Ford inherited on August 9.

He was not totally unfamiliar with it. Ford had been in the White House countless times as a congressman and from his position on the Hill had been privy to some of the inner workings of the executive branch. As Vice-President he had attended cabinet and National Security Council meetings, met agency heads and generally got the feel of the presidential scene. For all that, the real sense of power, its joys and its frustrations, is obscured from everybody but the person who resides at the center. Ford was there now. His initial response was that of a congressional leader seeking acceptance and consensus. He walked out of the East Room after taking the oath and began to touch the important bases of governmental authority.

Before anything else Ford met with the congressional leaders, a clear signal of his priority ratings. With their concurrence he scheduled a major address to a joint session of Congress and the nation for the following Monday. Then he moved back to the

President Ford takes Italy's President Giovanni Leone to his waiting limousine at the end of his visit. It was one of the first official visits of a head of state to President Ford. The two men had just completed their final discussions in the Oval Office, behind. Then they had walked slowly down the curving path toward Leone's motorcade, Secretary of State Henry Kissinger and the other White House and Italian aides coming on behind. It was a routine that has been going on for decades and doubtless will continue for many more. At the car door, Ford shook hands with his guests, then turned and walked back to the office with Kissinger, talking quietly about the results of the talks. On this afternoon there was one variation in the routine. While the President had been down on the drive, a thrush, totally unmindful of presidential power and protocol, had flown through the open office door and was flitting about the Oval premises. Aides went running around the office, trying to scare the bird back out of the door. President Ford watched with bemusement. "We have a crisis around here every hour," he said, chortling, as one of his military aides succeeded in coaxing the intruder out into the Rose Garden.

President Ford leans down to say good-by to a delegation of Polish officials after the signing of economic, trade and industrial agreements, the fruits of an earlier meeting with Polish Communist Chief Edward Gierek. This was a special gesture from a United States President. Normally, the session would have ended in the Cabinet Room with handshakes. In this instance, Ford took his visitors down the hall and out under the small portico on the West Wing of the White House. He not only saw that they were safely in their limousine, but bent down for a final warm farewell. No matter how hurried or how tense the moment, Ford never abandoned his intuitive good manners and politeness. Behind Ford, David Hume Kennerly, personal photographer to the President, gets off a quick shot or two as he dexterously clings to his cigarette. At the right is Naval Aide Stephen Todd. The two Marines are ceremonial door guards.

reception, where the champagne was still flowing and the happy guests waited to congratulate the new President. In the next few hours Ford was all over the White House. He walked into the press room and announced the appointment of his press secretary, Jerald F. terHorst, the talented and congenial bureau chief of the Detroit *Daily News*. TerHorst had known Ford since he first ran for Congress and terHorst was a political reporter on the Grand Rapids *Press*. Indeed, terHorst was even then putting the finishing touches on a Ford biography. Reporters jammed the room, shouted their greetings and congratulations to terHorst. Their relief at having a knowledgeable and friendly press secretary, after the months of deceit and bitterness dispensed by Ron Ziegler, Richard Nixon's press secretary, produced an uncharacteristic euphoria. The newsmen laughed too hard at Ford's jokes, grinned too much at terHorst to suit their own carefully prescribed role of friendly adversary. But it was a special moment. Ford declared that his administration would be an "open administration." It sounded good that afternoon. Ford, it was plain, felt he was among people he knew and respected. "We will have, I trust, the kind of rapport and friendship we've had in the past," he told them.

Back in the Oval Office, Ford counseled with his economic advisers and proclaimed, to no one's surprise, that inflation was the nation's number one enemy. He was briefed by the eager Henry Kissinger, the miraculous survivor of the five and a half Nixon years, who had done it by being first on the doorstep with the best information. Then, with Kissinger at his elbow, the new President stood for almost three hours as he greeted and chatted with each of Washington's resident ambassadors, sending to each man's country the assurance that American foreign policy would go on as it had.

Ford met, too, with a special team he had named to help him in the transition. It was headed by NATO Ambassador Donald Rumsfeld, who, sensing the approaching crisis, had flown to Washington on his own and

gone to Ford to ask if he could help. Rumsfeld was a long-time friend of Ford's and as a young Illinois congressman had helped to lead the revolt that toppled Charles Halleck and made Ford the minority leader. Pennsylvania's former governor and congressman, William Scranton, had flown in at Ford's request to serve. The other two men were former Virginia Congressman John O. Marsh and Interior Secretary Rogers Morton, another ex-congressman, and former chairman of the Republican National Committee. All were close friends of Ford's, and they had marched with him in previous political battles. Their task as outlined by Ford was to advise him on how to reorganize the White House staff, trim down its excess fat added by the Nixon bureaucrats. Under Nixon the White House staff had ballooned from 220 to 510 people. Ford also wanted a massive talent hunt so that he could get his own men not only in staff positions but in the cabinet and the agencies. Another Ford goal was to diminish the importance of the Office of Management and Budget, which under Nixon had virtually taken over direction of domestic policy from the cabinet officers.

When that momentous day was over sometime after 7 p.m., Gerald R. Ford, the thirty-eighth President of the United States, climbed into his limousine and headed back across the Potomac River for his home in Alexandria. The Nixons had left the White House so abruptly their things were not yet packed. It would be another ten days before the Fords could move in as a family. The light was fading as Ford made his way through the evening traffic, waving at astonished commuters. His car stopped at the traffic lights, slowed in the jam-ups, took its place in line for the turn-offs.

Ford was tired but jubilant. As he would admit later, even then his adrenaline was flowing. He liked being President. It is one of the persistent myths of the presidency that men shrink from the office because they are overwhelmed by its

prospects of power and undertake it only out of the most profound sense of public duty. In fact, they love it. Ford at that early moment was tasting the pleasures of pure power, the kind that only a few men taste in any given generation.

But Gerald Ford also was keeping his feet on the ground whence he came. At his split-level house neighbors and close friends had gathered for one last celebration before the presidency closed in totally and took him away, as inevitably it had to, into its own special place. Betty Ford had ordered a buffet supper of ham, lasagna and salad. There was more champagne, and before long the new President was out of his coat and tie and into an open soft shirt and slacks. "To the President," the smiling guests toasted. "To the first lady." It was after midnight when the Fords went to bed.

For those who had not already gotten the message that Ford would be a man very different from his coolly aloof predecessor, the fact came home with more force the day following the inauguration. Shortly after 7 a.m., the President of the United States appeared on his doorstep in baby-blue short pajamas, looking for the paper. The paper was late that morning and the unprotesting Ford went back to the preparation of his and son Steve's breakfast of juice and English muffins. As he left for the office he paused to sign autographs and to chat with reporters who loitered on the lawn. When would he move into the White House? Ford was questioned. "I didn't ask yesterday," he said. "I felt it would not be very appropriate." Then he was off and running again, picking up the loose and battered ends of the government, trying to form them into some sort of purposeful design.

At a cabinet meeting he asked his officers to stay on with him for the time being, rejecting "this business

The White House day is a ballet of people. They move in and out of the presidential orbit, conferring, phoning, reading and thinking. None is more important than the presidential staff members, four of whom are shown here. Secretary of State Henry Kissinger, left, stands quietly in the Oval Office one morning (the clock on the wall is not running), waiting for Ford to come to his desk. Under his arm Kissinger carries a summary of the state of the world. Each morning he brings this fresh report to Ford and briefs him on developments during the previous twenty-four hours. When Kissinger and Ford are both in town, the ritual varies little. Kissinger shakes hands with the President, says, "Good morning," sits down beside the presidential desk and starts his recitation. On this day in October, the two were talking about the White House position on the trade bill, held up in Congress over an amendment to force the Soviet Union to allow free emigration of Jews from the Soviet Union. In the center picture, Donald Rumsfeld, right, the chief of Ford's White House staff, gets updated by Major General Brent Scowcroft, a national security aide. When this picture was taken, in early October, Rumsfeld had been on the job only a few days, and not only did he have to familiarize himself with events but he also had to bring order out of what had been a formless period in White House routine. The two men talk in the doorway of Rumsfeld's office, which had been General Alexander Haig's and H. R. Haldeman's office in the Nixon days. Right: Alan Greenspan, the chairman of the Council of Economic Advisers, is shown walking from his secretary's office back into his own office. He is scanning the Washington Post in these minutes between phone calls and conferences with his assistants. Greenspan's spacious office is in the Executive Office Building, the huge gingerbread structure just west of the White House. The EOB houses vital parts of the executive apparatus such as the CEA.

L. William Seidman, left, the President's economic assistant, ponders a question in his office in the EOB. A millionaire accountant from Grand Rapids, Seidman was a long-time friend of Ford's who was lured to Washington when the power passed. He was at the center of the President's economic planning, the man who coordinated the work of all the economic advisers, made certain that Ford was presented the full range of ideas. William E. Timmons, right, was a brief holdover from Nixon's White House. He served as assistant for congressional affairs, counting votes and carrying White House messages to the Hill. Here, in Timmons' White House office on this October day, it was his job to get agreement from individual congressmen on the wording of a release on a presidential statement regarding meat prices and supply, and to set a time for simultaneous release in each man's home district. Behind Timmons is an autographed picture of Senate Republican Leader Hugh Scott, of Pennsylvania, and a scenic view of the Capitol at night. When not in the White House, Timmons was usually talking to legislators on the Hill. Bottom: The President's counsel, Philip Buchen, looks pensively at Fred Ward's camera. Buchen was a law partner of Ford's in Grand Rapids before Ford entered politics. Like Seidman, he answered Ford's call when Ford assumed the presidency. A kindly, thoughtful man, Buchen was Ford's principal strategist in the legalities of granting Richard Nixon the pardon. He talked with Fred at this moment about the difficulties in determining the ownership of presidential papers and the rights of the public and of Presidents, a problem complicated because at the time there was no law governing the matter, only the precedent, beginning with the first Presidents, that a man departing office could take his papers with him.

Two new, one old. Ron Nessen, below, Ford's second press secretary, takes lunch at his desk to catch up on his reading. He has just demolished the Mexican dish (enchiladas) from the White House mess and downed a Coors beer, a Ford favorite that suddenly became a White House staple. Nessen, a former NBC correspondent, who covered Ford when he was Vice-President, was appointed after Jerald F. terHorst, Ford's first press aide, quit in protest over the Nixon pardon. Nessen is shown in his office in the West Wing of the White House. Right: Dean Burch, one of Richard Nixon's political counselors, waits in the Oval Office for an appointment with Ford. Burch soon left the White House to return to private law practice. To his right against the wall is the Frederic Remington bronze "Bronco Buster." In the foreground is a corner of the President's desk and through the three-inch bulletproof glass, behind, is a glimpse of the South Lawn. Bottom: Speechwriter Robert Hartmann ponders the materials for a Ford speech. Pipes became a visible White House symbol in the Ford administration.

of pro-forma resignations." He emphasized again that he wanted his administration to be "open and candid." He urged the men and women who were there to adopt an "affirmative" approach with the press as one way to try to reunite the American people. Kissinger spoke for the cabinet in pledging that he would give "unflagging support and loyalty to you."

On the phone Ford reached out to all parts of the nation—to friends, even to traditional political enemies. He conferred again with Kissinger about the uneasy state of the world, and he called in his transition team for more discussion on how to get quickly engaged in his job. In this age of television it does not take long to establish the image of a man so mercilessly scrutinized as the President. As Ford worked away in these first hours, the glimpses of him were beamed over the country, and it was soon apparent that hate had died, the White House fortress was being dismantled.

On the Sunday following his assumption of power, Ford discarded another of the imperial practices of Nixon. There would be no church in the East Room, where the favored bearers of the Holy Word could preach to a sanitized and properly oriented audience. Ford chose to return to Immanuel Church on the Hill and the suburban Episcopal congregation with whom he had worshiped for the past twenty-six years.

When he had been tapped to be Ford's press secretary, terHorst had been typing out a prophetic piece for his paper. "Mr. Ford will not usher in a new era of Camelot or the big ranch scene," he wrote. "Few will probably acclaim Mr. Ford as the brightest intellect ever to sit behind a desk in the Oval Office. But it may be possible that some will acclaim him as one of the most decent, the most honest and the most candid Chief Executives of recent memory."

Ford played from that strength. On Monday night he journeyed to his old stamping grounds, the well of the House of Representatives, to confirm formally his intentions to work hard and offer reason and compassion to a country so battered and depressed. The gathering of the top people from all three branches of government to hear the President is a ritual of meaning in this democracy. The Capitol is aglow with lights, the black limousines slide in and out of the shadows, bearing men and women of power. The press galleries are jammed and the television cameras roam over the audience, picking out the famous faces. For Ford it was a homecoming. He knew the people on the floor as he walked down to their thunderous applause. He knew the ceremony and the expectations. He could feel the good will and the hope rise to engulf him. The ovation went on so long that Ford turned to his friend Speaker Carl Albert and said, "You're wasting good TV time." And Albert, not realizing the microphones were picking up his words, confided, "You know, I'm afraid I might have called you Jerry instead of Mr. President last night." Ford laughed.

"We have a lot of work to do," Ford began in his plain, no-nonsense voice. "Let's get on with it." His talk was a tour of the Ford mind, an outpouring of his thoughts of that moment in the language of the congressional cloakrooms and his native Michigan, designed to get "this country revved up and moving."

"As President, within the limits of basic principles, my motto towards the Congress is communication, conciliation, compromise and cooperation. . . . I do not want a honeymoon with you. I want a good marriage. . . . My office door has always been open and that is how it is going to be at the White House. Yes, congressmen will be welcome — if you don't overdo it."

There was laughter from people who once again felt close to the man at the other end of Pennsylvania Avenue. There were no rhetorical flourishes in Ford's speech. The language was simple and direct. It fit Ford. In that there was strength.

"I intend to listen. . . . I want to be sure that we are all tuned in to the real voice of America. . . . I believe in the First Amendment and the absolute necessity of a free press. . . . Inflation is our domestic public enemy number one. . . . A strong defense is the surest way to peace. . . . There will be no illegal tappings, eavesdropping, buggings, or break-ins by my administration. . . ."

The Ford testimony of basic decency, of firm belief in the tried rituals of the American system, rolled out into that packed chamber of eager believers. It was a splendid night for this nation, and Ford savored it fully, lingering after his address to shake every hand that was extended toward him.

On each of the following mornings Ford came to work in his big car down Interstate 95 and across the river, preceded by a police car and followed by four other vehicles, including a Secret Service escort and the press car. Ford buried himself in his paper as the small caravan sailed down the lane reserved for buses and car pools, greeted smiling commuters when the traffic bogged down.

There were a million pieces in the shattered mosaic of presidential authority and credibility. Ford hurried to put them back together, mixing his own warmth with the new authority of his office. When General Motors announced a 10 percent price increase for their 1975 automobiles, Ford fired off his first sharp criticism and won a temporary rollback. He called in his friends, like House whip Leslie Arends, who sat on a couch in the Oval Office, Ford on another, as the two remembered a few of their fine moments together on the Hill and looked ahead to Ford's days in the White House. Barry Goldwater, Arizona's crusty senator and national conservative voice, came by for a private chat. Melvin Laird was another friend who showed up for a few minutes with the President.

Office papers follow the President like some kind of plague. Left: Ford pauses to await his first ice-filled martini at the end of the office day. He is in the West Sitting Room on the second floor of the residence. On the table in front of him is the pile of night work which has followed him from the Oval Office. In his limousine, center, Ford continues his office ritual as he drives to the Bethesda Naval Hospital to see Mrs. Ford. When Fred Ward asked permission to come along in the car to photograph the President, Ford hesitated, explaining that he was behind in his reading and needed the few minutes to catch up. Fred promised silence during the ride. Indeed, after a short greeting, Ford put the documents on his lap and worked the entire thirty minutes in silence. At right, Ford signs a paper that has been delivered to him at night in the residence. There are no sacred hours for a President, no moment when he can be sure that the time will be his alone.

Ford ponders the troublesome matter of the Nixon tapes. Even though, when this picture was taken on October 10, Ford had pardoned Nixon and worked out the original deal for the tapes, the public controversy over the tapes continued. At this moment Ford was listening to then Attorney General William Saxbe and counsel Philip Buchen explain the problem. Ford was at his desk in the Oval Office. Before the tapes issue was finally taken up by Congress and the courts, Ford changed his position, keeping White House control of all of the controversial Nixon material.

The Soviet ambassador, Anatoly Dobrynin, who had cut short a vacation in the Soviet Union when Nixon resigned, was given assurances by Ford that détente would be his goal as much as it had been Nixon's. Ford promised to see if he could get the Senate to move on the trade reform bill, which would grant the Soviet Union better trading terms with the United States. Desperately in need of American technology, the Russians had pressed hard for the action ever since Nixon had agreed at the 1972 summit meeting to seek the change. A day later Ford invited the trade bill's harshest critics to one of those intimate White House breakfasts in the elegant family dining room. Nixon had never met directly with these men to talk about the bill. Washington's Henry Jackson, New York's Jacob Javits and Connecticut's Abraham Ribicoff eagerly accepted and over ham and eggs the senators poured out their feelings: in return for the special trade concessions the U.S. should insist that the Russians liberalize their laws regarding emigration rights and agree to end the harassment of Soviet Jews. It was the beginning of a compromise.

About the only thing that did not seem to work well for Ford in those early days was the telephone system. "I haven't figured this thing out yet," he said to one visitor as he fumbled with the buttons.

Ford took in stride the inevitable ripples that arise in a family living in in the presidential environment. When his son Mike, twenty-four, a divinity student, suggested publicly that Richard Nixon owed the American people a "total confession" of his role in the Watergate crimes, the news was received calmly by the President, who had a ready answer. "All my children have spoken for themselves since they first learned to speak," he said. "And not always with my advance approval. I expect that to continue in the future."

One morning the office of Congressman Charles Rangel, the New York Democrat who is chairman of the sixteen-member Black Caucus, received a phone call. "The President is calling," the voice said. Rangel's suspicious secretary turned to him and reported, "There's a call from somebody saying he's the President." Rangel picked up the line, and a familiar voice came through. "Hi, Charlie," boomed Ford. Rangel had asked that the President meet with the caucus, something Nixon had resolutely refused to do. Ford was delivering his approval of the idea in person.

Across Lafayette Park from the White House is the headquarters of the AFL-CIO, whose president, George Meany, had dedicated the previous months to running Richard Nixon out of office. His caustic thrusts had rumbled through the front door of the White House with such regularity that at times it seemed there would be no reconciliation with anybody remotely connected with Nixon. Ford asked him over and Meany went, cigar clamped firmly in place, frown deepened to show his skepticism. Meany, who has seen six Presidents come and go in his 23-year reign over the union forces, came away impressed, so much so that labor announced in a few days it was prepared to support Ford's idea for a new Cost of Living Council, an idea they had firmly opposed till then.

The parade marched on through the Oval Office. There was Democratic Senator Russell Long, of Louisiana, to talk over a new health care program that Ford wanted through Congress. When a representative of the United States mayors called up the President to ask which White House aide they should deal with about their problems, Ford said, "Start with me." They had a meeting. So did fourteen grateful governors, most of whom remembered the days when Richard Nixon would open a session with a few polite words, then excuse himself and turn the meeting over to one of his pious, uninformed minions. "It was like old times,"

reported West Virginia's Arch Moore. "We had the feeling we were most welcome."

When the Cyprus crisis erupted, Henry Kissinger moved close to Ford. The President spent hours being briefed, reading about the complex of violence embroiling Greece and Turkey. During one call to London, Henry Kissinger was in the Oval Office when he reached British Foreign Secretary James Callaghan, who in turn was in Prime Minister Harold Wilson's office at No. 10 Downing Street. "I am here in the Oval Office with the President and he would like a few words with you, Jim, and the Prime Minister." With that Ford and Wilson spent ten minutes exchanging mutual reassurances on the way they would react to the crisis. That small touch prompted the British officials to declare happily that Anglo-American relations had not been better since John Kennedy and Harold Macmillan used to ramble on with each other over the transatlantic line.

In odd moments Ford walked the few steps down the hall from his office into the small study that has been a favorite retreat of busy Presidents in the past. There Ford would take off his coat, perhaps loosen his tie, and do his private thinking. He had to come up with a vice-presidential nomination; out of the dozens of recommendations he had received, his own list was down to six and he was carefully pondering the choice. Once when Press Secretary terHorst came by to tell Ford that some papers were reporting he had narrowed the candidates from fifteen to only three, the President chortled and replied, "I'm glad you told me that. It'll save me a lot of time." In the end, his selection of Nelson Rockefeller was based more than anything on common sense. Rockefeller, though a man of some weaknesses and political liabilities, had more experience and talent than any of the others.

In this season of euphoria, enlarged to dangerous dimensions because of the Watergate hangover, if there were any doubts about the new President they were washed away in the instant joy. While no one claimed that Ford would provide brilliance or vision, the hope that his soundness would compensate for his failings grew to enormous proportions. And in fact, in almost every action there was a new glimpse of his character.

If one wanted courage, there was Ford's trip to Chicago, where, before the Veterans of Foreign Wars, he announced his intention to design an amnesty program for the estimated fifty thousand Vietnam draft dodgers and deserters. Before he went he had told his staff that he really wanted to bring the country together. "If I'm going to do that, then I've got to reach those kids who dodged the draft or deserted. I'm not for unlimited amnesty. Deserters can't go home scotfree when the kid next door might have been killed in Vietnam. Can't we fashion some way to let them earn their way back?" His people went to work and Ford flew to Chicago.

The aging veterans in their wilted suntans sat shocked as Ford declared that he intended to "bind up the nation's wounds," and one step would be to let those who had fled the United States to escape military service "come home, if they want to work their way back." Standing straight, his mouth in a firm line, Ford said he would throw "the weight of my presidency into the scales of justice on the side of leniency. . . . I reject amnesty, and I reject revenge."

In his shirt sleeves, flying back from Chicago on Air Force One, Ford was resolute. "You can't talk about healing unless you're going to use it in the broadest context. . . . I thought that the right audience would be an audience that might be difficult. It would

have been a little cowardice, I think, if I'd picked an audience that was ecstatic."

No sooner had he finished that task than he summoned House and Senate leaders, cabinet members and the press into his presence. With Nelson Rockefeller at his side, he told the world that he had found his nominee for Vice-President, "a tough call for a tough job." It was simple, short and direct. Then back to work.

The nomination of Rockefeller, however, started speculation that Ford would be a candidate in 1976, a perennial Washington guessing game. Press Secretary terHorst was bombarded with questions on Ford's possible candidacy. He caught the President at the end of the day and walked with him through the Rose Garden toward the residence. "It's this way," Ford explained. "As I told Governor Rockefeller, I have changed my mind because conditions have changed. I didn't think I would run. Now I probably will run." TerHorst, who had reported the Nixon years, was still not quite ready for his own boss's candor. "Is it all right to put that out?" he asked. "I don't see why not," said Ford. "Why should we pretend?" No reason, agreed terHorst, who told reporters exactly that and for a second relished their amazement.

And humor? Well, it was not quite like Bob Hope or the belly-shaking stories of Lyndon Johnson. But it could be found by the people who wanted to find it, which was almost everybody. Looking across his desk at the heir to countless millions, a man who has lived in unmatched luxury all his life, the President ribbed Nelson Rockefeller. "You know," he said, referring to the drafty eighty-one-year-old house consigned to Vice-Presidents, "you are going to have to live in the old Admiral's House. But you can visit your lovely home on Foxhall Road on weekends." (Rockefeller has long had his own Washington estate.)

There was some fun mixed with the long hours of work. The first week ended with one of the liveliest White House parties seen in years. It was for King Hussein and Queen Alia of

Jordan. Though hastily planned and executed, the evening was a smashing success, due more than anything to the attitude of Betty and Jerry Ford. "This house has been like a grave," said Mrs. Ford. "I want it to sing." Protocol dictates that no guest can leave a presidential party until the first couple go up to their private quarters. The Nixons, partly out of such consideration and partly because they did not care that much for dancing, often left state dinners just after the entertainment. It was not going to be that way with the Fords. "I'm just going to tell the guests they can leave whenever they want to," Betty Ford declared. "Nobody's going to get us off the dance floor at ten o'clock." They didn't.

Ford danced again and again with the lovely Queen and she proclaimed the event "a swinging party." The King did his smooth bit with Betty Ford as the champagne flowed, and the old mansion warmed up as it used to when Lyndon Johnson steered his partners over the polished floors. Once royalty departed, Ford and his wife came back to the dancing. At one point the President paired off with Cindy Nessen, the Korean-born wife of NBC newsman Ron Nessen, and while the guests shouted and applauded, Ford improvised his way through "Bad, Bad Leroy Brown."

Once again there was evidence that the old White House barriers had been dropped, that the enemies lists had been consigned to the fire. Among the dinner guests were World Bank President Robert McNamara, John Kennedy's Secretary of Defense, who had been deliberately snubbed through all of Nixon's years; anti-Nixon Congressman Pete McCloskey of California; and Carroll Kilpatrick, a reporter for the Washington *Post*, the White House's very special *bête noire* during the time of Watergate. In the joy of the moment, liberal Republican Senator Mark Hatfield, of Oregon, grinned and shouted out what was felt by everyone. "Happy New Year." It was still August.

A Style Emerges

He stood in the ornate Akasaka Palace in Japan in November 1974, leaning over slightly to catch the words of the thirteen-year-old boy scout in the white sneakers. Second-class scout Haruhiko Murase from Tokyo had for the President of the United States a red, white and blue neckerchief, its slide decorated with a picture of Mount Fuji. Gerald Ford took the neckerchief, tried to slip it over his head and got it hung up for a second on his ears. Haruhiko looked anxious, but Ford grinned, tugged the neckerchief into place, then turned and gave the boy the left-handed scout grip. It came from deep down inside Ford, the first eagle scout to be President of the United States. The little guy in front of Ford was gloriously spellbound.

When Ford told the small group of Japanese scouts and leaders that scouting had meant a great deal to him, there were no nonbelievers in the room. "I'm proud of the friends I made in scouting. I'm proud of the examples they set...scouting stands for the best in people and ideals and that is good for all mankind." Much that Ford believes and much that guides his actions today in the presidency is rooted in what he learned as a scout.

One of the things is sportsmanship. Ford plays hard, but when the contest is over and it is time to walk off the field, the battle is left behind. He sat one night in the Oval Office shortly after he had assumed power and explained that life was a continuing contest, but there came a moment in every skirmish when it was time to drop the grudges and move on. He had founded his successful congressional career on the idea that good fights did not make permanent enemies. Nor had he ever been vindictive, he said. You did your best, then you walked off satisfied. These old ideas of friendly combat are very much part of Ford. And when he sits

in the White House and makes decisions, they bubble up out of the stuff that was formed in South High School, Grand Rapids, Michigan, class of 1930. Ford played center and was team captain when South High won the city and state championships. Every year since, at Thanksgiving, the thirty members of that squad have convened for a reunion of the "30-30 Club," as they called it. In 1974, at the President's invitation, they gathered at the White House, and before the brunch and the back slapping were over it had turned into a testimonial to the constant inspiration of Gerald Ford back when the Trojans were rolling over all their opposition. "He came to me a spindly, awkward kid," recalled the team's coach, Clifford Gettings, now seventy-two and a real estate man. " 'What position shall I play?' he asked. I said, 'Center,' and he's been in the center of things ever since. He had a lot of drive. He always had a football in his hand and must have practiced centering that ball day and night....I never saw him make a bad pass. He was All-City three years and All-State in his senior year."

On that 1974 Thanksgiving Day, Silas McGee, an end and the only black on the old team, went around grinning and embracing his teammates and remembering they called the President "Junie" because he was Gerald R. Ford, Jr. "I don't care what he became," said McGee. "He was always a guy I loved. He was always down to earth, like the rest of this group." Leon Joslin, the other Trojan end, had his story too. Ford had been so dedicated to football, the team and winning that he had persuaded the boys to practice before the season. "We all went up to his stepfather's cabin in the hills," Joslin said, "and he acted as coach as we drilled our tails off."

Another early-laid foundation stone in Ford's life was the church. Unlike Johnson and Nixon, Gerald Ford went to church regularly before he got to the White House. He knew the verses from Proverbs on which his hand was resting when he took the

presidential oath. Back at the church after his inaugural, he sang the hymns with his accustomed gusto: "Blessings abound where'er he reigns. The prisoner leaps to loose his chains; The weary find eternal rest; And all the sons of want are blest."

On the night he talked to Congress he said, "We all need God's sure guidance," and that theme was one he repeated in many of his public and private declarations. When the storm about pardoning Richard Nixon broke over Ford, his former Grand Rapids law partner, Philip Buchen, who came to the White House to be Ford's counsel, sent around some words of support from a Grand Rapids pastor, knowing that they would have special significance for Ford. "Forgive when you can," the Reverend Duncan Littlefair, of the Grand Rapids Foundation Street Church, had said. "Mercy and forgiveness cannot be weighed, measured and balanced and counted— they must always be free, unearned and undeserved." Buchen knew his man. Ford mentioned the sermon to visitors who wondered about the wisdom of granting a pardon.

Scouts. Football. Sunday school. In the long view of history they recede almost to footnotes in the biographies but they help to form the core of any man, even of one who becomes President. There are fewer changes after those first formative years than many would like to believe. I have watched five Presidents in the Oval Office and I have come to believe with increasing fervor that how they conduct the presidency can be traced directly back to early influences. Around the White House press room back in the Johnson days, we used to talk about the President's "Alamo syndrome," which was our shorthand to explain each new round of Vietnam escalation. At least a few of us were convinced that his machismo, nurtured along the Pedernales River just sixty miles from the Alamo, was more important in his

The television quartz lights blaze as the President and Mrs. Ford head for the East Room to form a reception line for Austria's Chancellor Dr. Bruno Kreisky. They had just finished cocktails with the Chancellor in the private quarters and had come down the stairs, where they posed for the official picture. At this moment they stride toward the East Room, the still photographers busy in the foyer. It was at this state dinner that it became clear that the White House hate lists of the Nixon days had been abolished. Among many guests who had not been there for years were Supreme Court Justice William O. Douglas and his wife. The tough old Democrat had been a special target of the Nixon administration, Ford himself having once led the attack on the Hill to have Douglas impeached. All was forgiven—by both men—on this night.

The President's dog, Liberty, waits patiently for a little attention as Ford eats his lunch, left. The lunch was the usual cottage cheese with Worcestershire sauce and a green salad. The desktop lunch is not a fixed Ford habit, but when pressed for time or when Mrs. Ford is not in the White House, the President resorts to the White House mess service. While he ate on this day, he read papers on his desk. Once finished, Ford, right, with little more than a glance at stewards hurrying the tray away, leaned back in his chair with his reading, giving Liberty

a reassuring scratch on the neck. Ford's pipe equipment can be seen on the stand at the right. Once when photographer Ward came into the office, Ford was just straightening up, face red, after stamping out a fire in the wastebasket in the foreground. He had tapped out pipe ashes that were still glowing, then noticed the blaze just as Shirley Temple Black came into the Oval Office to see Ford before going to Ghana as ambassador.

final decision to fight than our treaty commitments or the counsel he got from his generals, which was not unanimously in favor of massive intervention. In his private moments after a drink or two, he more or less confirmed it. He would look around at the people in front of him and say, "It's just like the Alamo. Somebody should have helped those Texans. By God, I'm going to Vietnam."

Earlier, John Kennedy had echoed old Joe Kennedy's teachings with very little modification. "I figure," he told me one night, "if you are willing to settle for second best that is the way it will be." Out of that preoccupation with being first, I suspect, came the motivation to "bear any burden" in the pursuit of peace and, of course, the impulse to conquer the moon. I sat one day in the Gettysburg office of Dwight Eisenhower. In a few months he would be dead, but for that small interlude he was the old Ike, full of wonder at how far he had come in this world, still grateful for what this nation had done for him. He talked of his home and of West Point, and how he had never had to learn much more than they had taught him to make his way. And before him, Harry Truman ("Four Eyes," as he was called, according to Merle Miller) was much the same in the White House as he had been when he was a kid (he read every book in the Independence, Missouri, library), when he was a farmer (he read Cato's treatise on agriculture in the original Latin), when he was a county official (he accounted for every penny he spent) and when he was a senator (he studied Caesar's commentaries for political insights).

It was true with Nixon too. There is some combination of heredity and circumstance there, some deep injury in family or community that brought about his tragedy. His success, too, can be calculated from those begin-

nings, when he heard the distant trains and imagined great empires and great men and believed implicitly the Horatio Alger stories he read.

James David Barber, a political scientist at Duke University, has done what I could never do in my hurried observations while running after these peripatetic men. His book *The Presidential Character* details his own conclusions about the why and how of Presidents going all the way back to George Washington. And while he, too, realizes there is no certain way to judge the reasons for these men's doing the things they did, or why men now on the scene, both in the White House and contending for the title, may take certain actions, he presents a convincing case connecting the characters of these men with the personalities, education, hobbies, successes and failures of their mothers and fathers.

Once the men moved into the presidency, their character set the tone in the office, shaping its meaning and its manner of operation. That aura seeped out into the executive branch and ultimately into the nation. It is Barber's view, for example, that country squire George Washington never lost his love of Mount Vernon and conceived, therefore, a nation of rooted people given to developing their skills on the farms and in the villages of their forebears. He was a man of hearth and home. Washington brought a period of conservatism when the foundling nation desperately needed it. After the upheaval of the Revolution, America required a few years to pause and collect its strength before moving west and developing its endowment. Jefferson, the man of the restless, probing mind, passed his curiosity on to the nation, and not only made the Louisiana Purchase but sent Lewis and Clark to see the new land on one of the greatest explorations man has ever undertaken.

Even in college, Barber found, Woodrow Wilson pursued his ideals relentlessly. It was a trait that would establish his lofty rhetoric on the pages of history but yield few con-

crete results in his time. Wilson's dream of the League of Nations was destroyed in his intransigent battles with the Senate. After that Wilson himself collapsed.

And if the impact of the presidency on the country has always been immense, now it is even greater—and almost instant, since television acts as a magnifier on the institution. One night, following a difficult day, I asked John Kennedy whether there was anything that surprised him about being President. He replied that while he had practically grown accustomed to living with the idea of nuclear weapons or the possibility that he might have to send troops to fight, what constantly amazed him was the powerful effect his appearance, his actions and his remarks seemed to have. Every utterance, every gesture had immense impact. A chance remark could influence thousands to act. Kennedy had recently suggested (mostly in jest) that, like the U.S. Marines, Americans should take fifty-mile hikes to get in shape. Literally hundreds of thousands of persons promptly hit the trails, and the American Medical Association nervously suggested caution for those not accustomed to such exertion. Lyndon Johnson once marveled that if he had a cold and his complexion wasn't quite right, the stock market could drop five points. Harry Truman spotted that power early and was, for the most part, very respectful of it. He said that criticism by a President was a devastating thing and any President had to be extremely careful not to ruin a person's life by a casual or thoughtless response to the countless irritations that beset a Chief Executive.

Touch football became a national fad because the Kennedys played. JFK's interest in reading, particularly history, spurred a mild national revival. Lyndon Johnson gave the barbecue currency in the Northeast, where it had rarely penetrated before he set off the signal by having a huge cookout at the White House. Eisenhower inspired thousands of elderly men and women to try oil painting, and the fact that Richard Nixon had seen the movie *Patton* three times gave it an inestimable box office boost. A President's belief (or nonbelief) in a balanced budget has its effects on people. And his sense of humor influences the nation's outlook. How he rears his family, treats his wife, spends his spare time, cast a long shadow into all homes. And finally his morals, his sense of right and wrong, set a standard of conduct that touches the national soul.

Our political system often obscures the true dimensions of the men who seek the presidency. The campaigns are blurs of flying trips, hastily conceived and written speeches, bands, balloons and hoopla that may give some idea of a man's energy and his facility at managing words and crowds but reveal little of the inner urges that come from seldom examined beginnings. Political talk all too frequently bears little relationship to subsequent action. Kennedy's brave words about opposing any foe in the interests of freedom rang hollow when the Berlin wall went up in the summer of 1961 and we did nothing but offer verbal protests. LBJ went around the nation in 1964 saying he was not about to send American boys to fight Asian battles and we took him at his word, totally ignorant of the pride that would never allow him to back away from such a confrontation. Richard Nixon was a creature of opportunity, and before long his words became meaningless. One year an unbalanced budget was declared immoral; the next year he hailed it as the salvation of the national economy. He proclaimed himself one month to be philosophically opposed to wage and price controls; the next month he staggered everybody by imposing them. What ruled in those matters, and of course with Watergate, was the inner person of the President, which, as we can see now, had no fixed moral compass and no

established values except as needed to preserve power and position.

Gerald Ford early had his days of baffling contradiction and almost overnight, thanks to television's unblinking eye, those people who had lured themselves into believing once again found themselves teetering on the brink of a credibility gap. A casual press conference indication by Ford that he would let the judicial process run its course with Richard Nixon seemed a mockery two weeks later when on a Sunday morning the President suddenly announced that he would pardon Nixon of all Watergate crimes, even before any possible indictments or trials. His decision was arrived at in such secrecy that his pledge to run an open administration also appeared open to challenge. And then in the campaign of 1974, when he reverted to old-fashioned congressional hyperbole and told the nation that to elect more Democrats would threaten peace and prosperity, it was obvious once again that what he said could not be the sole measure of the new man. To get some sense of what Ford might do in the future, one had to take a searching look back at what made him.

Gerald Rudolph Ford, Jr., was born Leslie Lynch King, Jr., on July 14, 1913, not in Grand Rapids, Michigan, but in Omaha, Nebraska. His mother, the former Dorothy Gardner, had married Leslie King, a Western wool dealer. The marriage was apparently bad from the start; within two years the couple divorced and Dorothy, a good-looking brunette in her twenties, was back in Grand Rapids. She soon attracted the eye of an earnest young bachelor around town named, Gerald R. Ford. They met at an Episcopalian church social, and in 1916 they married. Ford not only adopted young Leslie but gave him his name. His background was kept secret from the boy for seventeen years. One day, while working at a local restaurant, according to Jerald terHorst's biography of the President, Ford looked up and noticed a man standing in front of the candy counter. As Ford told it to terHorst: "He stood there

for a long time—he was a stranger— and finally, he walked across to me and said, 'Leslie, I'm your father.' I was a little startled to be addressed as Leslie. Then he said, 'Yes, I am your father. I was divorced from your mother. Would you go out to lunch with me?' I took off my apron and we went out to lunch." That night he heard the full story from his mother and stepfather. Ford saw King only one other time and that was when he was a law student at Yale. The experience left a small scar. But no permanent injury. He was Gerald Ford's son in heart and mind if not in blood.

The elder Ford was a paint salesman who prospered in the first years of the young man's life. Grand Rapids was a thriving center of furniture manufacturing. Soon there were younger half brothers, a family touring car and a comfortable house on Madison Avenue in an established part of the small city. There was money enough for occasional vacations in Florida, but it was still necessary for the young Fords to work for pocket money. Ford, Sr., gave his stepson a respect for hard work, an understanding of community obligation and a love of athletics. Though the elder Ford's career as a businessman rode the roller coaster of those years from boom to near bust, he had a solid reputation among his neighbors for character, good works and humility. Remember, he told his stepson, someone else can always do the job better than you.

In 1929 the senior Ford formed a small paint and varnish company. The family moved into a new home in East Grand Rapids, the fashionable section of town, and Jerry became star center on the South High School football team. That was also the year of the stock market crash, and America slid into the Depression. The Ford business venture almost went under. The new house proved to be

In the key White House offices, the Secret Service furnishes a computerized readout on the exact location of their main charges. On October 29, the President (1) was in the Oval Office. Mrs. Ford (2) was out of the White House but in Washington. So was daughter Susan (3). Son Steve (4) was at a ranch in Lolo, Montana, and son Jack (5) was in school at Utah State University, Logan. The third son, Michael, (6) was in Gordon-Cornwell Theological Seminary, Essex, Massachusetts. Vice-President Nelson Rockefeller (7) at the time of the picture was in New York and the ubiquitous Henry Kissinger (8) was in Bangladesh. When these persons move, the new information is fed into the system and the readout changes automatically. Far left: The President goes over his calendar safely behind his desk in the Oval Office.

Left above: Speechwriter Hartmann has produced a first draft of a Ford speech. The President, who has studied it, is explaining his corrections to Hartmann. Most corrections on this mid-October occasion had to do with proper phrasing, Ford telling Hartmann, "I would say it this way" or "This doesn't sound exactly like me." Left below: Press Secretary Nessen gets briefed before he goes out into the Press Room to brief White House reporters in the morning. Nessen's data-gathering routine begins about 8 a.m. at the senior White House staff meeting where he picks up information on White House events. He then goes back to meet in his office with his own staff, developing probable questions of the day and suggested answers. His next stop is the President's office. In this picture he is presenting potential questions and answers, getting Ford's corrections and instructions.

During his days on the Hill as minority leader, Ford became known as a back patter and arm gripper, a warm bear of a man who liked to make contact with the flesh. As President he did not change. Opposite page, right: at a black-tie dinner for congressional retirees, he pauses with North Carolina's Senator and Mrs. Sam Ervin. Though in one sense Ford joined the opposition when he went into the White House, he vowed not to lose his relationships with the men on the Hill. In his first months, at least, he kept that pledge, even though there were some spirited arguments over policy. Opposite page, left: Ford puts an arm around Vermont's retiring Senator George Aiken while he talks to Aiken's wife. Left: Ford automatically gives a waitress his political grip at an Ohio Republican rally in Cleveland. At this moment Ford was all pol, wearing one of his WIN ("Whip Inflation Now") buttons and reaching for almost every hand within arm's length. The amused man on the right is Ohio's Senator Robert Taft.

too much of a burden, and the family moved to more modest quarters, but young Jerry still played on the South High team even though he had to take a fifty-minute bus ride to and from the school.

He led his team, coaxing a little more out of them, and going that extra distance himself, always trying a little harder. "The center was not just the guy who stuck the ball in the quarterback's hands," he explains. "Every center snap truly had to be a pass between the legs, often leading the tailback who was in motion and in full stride when he took the ball. I don't mean to be critical, but I think that is why you see so many bad passes from center on punts and field goals nowadays—they don't have to do it enough. I must have centered the ball 500,000 times in high school and later in college."

With an athletic scholarship and a bunch of odd jobs, Jerry Ford attended the University of Michigan. He was still a good center and a solid B student, spending his summers as a ranger in Yellowstone National Park.

Ford was voted Michigan's most valuable player in 1935, his last year, and went off into an uncertain world thankful for having had the chance to play football. "My football experiences helped me many times to face a tough situation in World War II or, in the rough and tumble of politics, to take action and make every effort despite adverse odds." Indeed, he often used gridiron metaphors in reference to his political career. "I've tried to be a good blocker and tackler for the running back who carries the ball," he once remarked.

Ford turned down offers to play pro ball with the Green Bay Packers and the Detroit Lions. Instead, he took a job at Yale as an assistant line coach, junior varsity coach and coach of the boxing team. The new position, which paid $2,400 a year, gave him a chance to stay close to football and attend

law school, an aspiration that had been building for some time. As for boxing, he confessed he knew almost nothing. "I boxed lightweights and coached heavyweights," he said, laughing. His real battle was with his professors and his books. At first his scholastic advisers did not think he could work full time and attend law school. He was allowed to attend two courses on a trial basis. He did so well that he was given permission to take on a full load but with a warning that he was on a fast academic track. He finished in the top third of his law class of 1941 and even found time to have some fun.

Shortly after entering Yale he had met Phyllis Brown, a beauty from Connecticut College for Women. They skied and partied, the handsome, stolid Ford making an impressive backdrop for Miss Brown's wit and vivaciousness. When she got out of school she went to New York and began a career as a model, then persuaded Ford to invest a thousand dollars in a new model agency to be run by Harry Conover. Ford himself was lured into modeling by his sparkling girl friend. *Look* magazine featured the pair in a picture story about a Vermont skiing weekend, complete with photos of spills, a fireside massage and a good-by kiss. Ford still has a copy of the magazine and told terHorst wryly, "It's not something you flaunt around the house." In 1942 Ford (by then in a Navy uniform) posed with Miss Brown for the cover of *Cosmopolitan* magazine. That was the beginning of the end of Ford's modeling career, his association with the Conover Agency and, finally, his close friendship with Miss Brown. There was more serious work to be done, including a war.

He had returned to Grand Rapids in 1941 and had begun to practice law with his college roommate Philip Buchen. Politics interested him, too, even as the war in Europe grew. He and a group of young men around the city began to hold discussions about breaking up the local machine. Then came Pearl Harbor, and Ford promptly enlisted in the Navy as an ensign. First he was sent to the University of

North Carolina to help get new recruits into good physical shape. But, with the fighting growing on two fronts, that was not something Ford enjoyed. So he requested sea duty and finally got it. He was assigned to the aircraft carrier U.S.S. *Monterey* in the South Pacific and was under enemy fire in several major battles. His worst scare came during a typhoon when he was almost washed overboard, landing perilously on a catwalk beneath him. The *Monterey*, said Ford later, was a lucky ship.

Ford was mustered out a lieutenant commander at thirty-two and returned to Grand Rapids and the practice of law, eager now for the good life. He played a lot of golf, saw a lot of football games and took out the girls. He was a joiner, too, and became a member of almost every civic group handy. He joined the American Legion, the Veterans of Foreign Wars, the Masons, the Elks. He kept in close touch with the boy scouts, still relishing the pride he had felt in reaching eagle scout as a boy.

Through his college days and early in the war, Ford had been a good son of the middle lands. His idea of the world was that nations should leave each other alone. He was, in short, an isolationist, to the extent that he even thought about it. But the war showed him that the world was not as simple as he had perceived it on the prairies, and he became convinced that America had a leadership role to perform. Ford's conversion fit nicely with the desires of another Grand Rapids man who had changed his mind about the responsibilities of the United States in the world. He was Senator Arthur Vandenberg, the genial editor who had gone to Washington as a Fortress America man and then had made a dramatic switch during the war to furnish Roosevelt the bipartisan support that was essential to unify the American effort. Vandenberg did not stop at that. With the Republicans in control of the Senate after the war, he became chairman of the Foreign Relations Committee. He also became

The President dances with Mrs. Gierek in the White House foyer following the state dinner.

a founder of the United Nations and led the drive within the Senate for United States membership. The old senator was a convert to Truman's Marshall Plan, the program of American aid for a Europe devastated by a decade of war.

Vandenberg had a great irritant in his new role as statesman. Bartel J. Jonkman, congressman from Michigan's Fifth, which included Grand Rapids, was a top Republican on the House Foreign Affairs Committee, and somehow the new view of the world that Vandenberg and Ford shared had passed him by. At every opportunity Jonkman attacked the Marshall Plan, warning darkly that it was nothing more than taking good capitalistic dollars to support foreigners who were likely to be wooed away by the socialists.

The young veterans just moving into politics in Grand Rapids had had their fill of Jonkman too. With some discreet signals from Vandenberg, the insurgents asked Ford to tackle Jonkman in the Republican primary in 1948. The odds in that old-line Republican district were formidable and Ford hesitated, then plunged in, sensing something stirring in the post-war world not reflected in the traditional Republican philosophy of western Michigan. It was not the most brilliant campaign ever waged by a young man but it may have been one of the most determined. From dawn to dusk Ford worked the supermarkets, the Main Streets and the Rotary halls. Whatever Ford did, he did it right. He beat Jonkman handily in the primary and went on to swamp his Democratic opponent in the November election.

Meanwhile, young Ford had acquired a bride, Betty Bloomer Warren, a divorced fashion coordinator of a local department store. She was an extraordinary person who had once danced with Martha Graham's modern-dance troupe in New York City. They had dovetailed a small wedding between Ford's primary and the general elections, purposely keeping it low key

so as not to arouse the devout Dutchmen of the Fifth District to question Betty's previous life. One thing remembered from the wedding, according to terHorst, was the concern of Ford's mother over the fact that the groom had come to the wedding in a gray pin-stripe suit and the same dusty brown shoes he had used for campaigning earlier in the day. Perhaps that incident foreshadowed the time twenty-six years later when Ford would stride down the red ceremonial carpet in Japan as President of the United States, his trousers three inches too short.

In Washington Ford instantly saw the wisdom in the House adage: To get along, go along. He joined the team, spent his spare hours on the floor watching debate and parliamentary maneuver. Proving himself a good student, in his second term he was awarded a seat on the powerful Appropriations Committee and soon became an expert on defense spending.

He applied the same effort to serving his home district. Almost every week he managed to get back to Grand Rapids for one thing or another. In his later House years, the local Republicans would insist that there was almost nobody in Ford's district for whom he had not done a favor or two.

In 1964 Ford was ready for one of those unexpected opportunities that come in politics. The House Republican contingent had been seriously thinned in the massive Democratic landslide against presidential candidate Barry Goldwater, and the G.O.P. young Turks saw their present leader Charles Halleck, the Indiana "gut fighter," as a symbol of retreat. Offering Ford as their candidate, they eked out a narrow six-vote victory and suddenly Ford was a national figure.

Not the least of his new duties was to be straight man on the "Ev and Jerry Show," a weekly Republican rebuttal to Lyndon Johnson's "Great Society." Illinois Senator Everett Dirksen's delightful rococo oratory was the centerpiece of each performance, but the face of Gerald Ford soon became familiar in every hamlet. Ford seemed made for his new job on the floor. "No man's light will be hidden under

a bushel," he announced to his fellow Republicans. Then he lived up to it, giving credit where it was due, stepping into the background at every opportunity. He made friends in both parties through his self-effacing, modest ways and thereby increased his influence in the congressional arena. "It's the damnedest thing," mused a Democrat one day. "Jerry just puts an arm around a colleague or looks him in the eye, says, 'I don't need your vote,' and gets it."

Ford became known on the Hill as a "hugger and a patter," a big, beefy guy who would squeeze an arm or slap a back and give the recipient a feeling of being something special. "Jerry is an open tactician," said one of his Republican colleagues. "He doesn't look for clever ways to sneak in behind you. He does the obvious, which is usually common sense."

His loyalty to the party line was held up for praise by the stalwarts. But it was another trait that would raise questions when Ford entered the White House. Did Ford have a mind of his own, it was asked, any philosophical moorings that could be defined? In the House he had marched by the numbers so resolutely that he voted by rote, or so it seemed, against almost all Democratic legislation of import. He voted against subsidized housing and aid to education, Medicare, the Johnson antipoverty program, minimum wage bills. In 1973 he was one of seventy congressmen who voted to sustain all Richard Nixon's vetoes. Those few times Ford did seem to waver, he ended up more conservative than the White House. He voted against using any of the highway trust funds for mass transit systems, which may have some logic in Michigan (the auto state), but is not the stand anyone in the White House has taken for years. For all Ford's open-mindedness and his willingness to study events and issues, there still was a good deal of that fierce, self-made-man sort of reaction in Ford. "If Jerry saw a hungry child,

Ford gives singer Vicki Carr a buss after her numbers at the dinner for Austria's Chancellor Bruno Kreisky.

The President goes over a speech in October on his way to Kansas City aboard Air Force One. The plane is a functioning White House in the sky with many of the marvelous services that are furnished presidents on the ground. Travel is so much a part of any Chief Executive's routine that conferences and study time are often scheduled on the plane. Ford in this picture sits at the table in his cabin. There is another large seat across from him, a couch across the aisle at his left. Behind Ford is a small lounge and a private lavatory. The long corridor to the right is the passageway from the flight deck and the communications center back to the area for guests, staff, security agents and press. In Nixon's time the door with the presidential seal on it was almost always kept closed. Nixon demanded solitude. Ford almost inevitably travels with the door open. He can see through to the pilot's cabin from this position. Presidential planes have figured prominently in modern history. John Kennedy held his final strategy session on an earlier Air Force One before he met Nikita Khrushchev in the historic Vienna summit meeting in 1961. Lyndon Johnson was sworn in on the same plane at Dallas in 1963, then flew to Washington, with Kennedy's body aboard. Some of Johnson's Asian policy was devised while he was airborne in Asian skies. The plane that Ford uses flew Nixon back to San Clemente and in midflight President Nixon became ex-President Nixon, another momentous moment in the clouds.

he would give the kid his lunch," said A. Robert Kleiner, a Democrat from Ford's district. "But he can't see that voting against the school lunch program is depriving millions of kids of food."

But for almost every such question there was a redeeming feature that critics and friends alike could call to mind. Only once did Ford seem to lose judgment in his role as leader. After Nixon's two Supreme Court nominees, Haynsworth and Carswell, had been bitterly rejected by the Senate, Ford, with encouragement from the White House, counterattacked by calling for impeachment of Supreme Court Justice William O. Douglas, a liberal and a thirty-six-year court veteran. Ford criticized Douglas's $12,000 annual fee from a foundation, his writing in *Evergreen Review,* in which Douglas, according to Ford, seemed to sanction revolution in America. At one point Ford waved a copy of the magazine and noted that the Douglas article was in the company of photographs of nude women. In this uncharacteristic tirade Ford propounded an axiom of congressional behavior that would come back to haunt him and Nixon. Ford declared that an impeachable offense was what a House majority said it was. There was much truth in that statement, but when Nixon faced impeachment Ford vainly fought the same view. When the Douglas storm settled, a chastened Ford looked back and saw that he had gone too far. "Impeachment would have been too harsh," he said. Three months after he became President, Ford asked Douglas and his wife to a state dinner and the two men shook hands warmly. For both it was over and done, one of those interludes in the affairs of the government that keep proving there are few permanent enemies in politics.

In Ford's early weeks in office it was plain there was little chance for innovation. His task was to hold the nation together and to begin the healing. Ford's past holds little to indicate that he will be a massively creative President. In Grand Rapids he accepted the rituals of religion, school, family and the playing field, honoring them and enlarging them with his own special talent. On the Hill, Ford was an arbitrator, a compromiser, a manipulator of ideas and men. He did not produce new plans or call for anything beyond the system. His votes were mostly against bills, not for new thoughts. His talent was important in that context. But when he went down Pennsylvania Avenue the world changed for Ford, and the ultimate evaluation of whether or not he understood what happened will be written by future historians.

There were times in those early days when Ford still seemed to be the minority leader, standing beside the flow of ideas and grabbing the ones he wanted, rejecting the others, nudging things a bit to try to produce an agreement here and a deal there. At a press conference in December, when asked about a gasoline tax increase, Ford cited a public opinion poll to back up his own doubts. The poll showed that 81 percent of Americans were against the idea. "I think I'm on pretty solid ground," Ford asserted. For that moment, at least, it seemed as if he were back in the well of the House, calculating consensus. Indeed, Ford seemed to be a bemused observer, standing to one side and offering his opinion as others debated. Criticism of this remark, like others, surprised Ford. It was as if he said, "Who, me?" when people turned to him for something besides comment.

The Grand Rapids instincts were easily detectable when Ford was limned by the harsh presidential light. One of his first acts was to summon Philip Buchen as his White House counsel. Buchen, crippled with polio, is a Phi Beta Kappa who once thought he wanted to be a writer. Another Grand Rapids man, L. William Seidman, a millionaire accountant, was brought in to become the President's assistant for economic affairs. Seidman was a Phi Beta Kappa from Dartmouth College who had gone back to Grand Rapids to prosper and been a friend of Jerry Ford's from the start of Ford's political career.

After dinner in Air Force One, Ford lights his pipe and sips tea, two routines that are part of his existence, earthly or airborne. Beside the President is a White House phone, with which he can call any place in the world with little more effort than if he were at his desk in the Oval Office. Hanging on the back of Ford's chair is the special flight jacket, with its presidential seal, that the plane crew keeps aboard for the President.

Ford, in line with his administration's era of openness, allows ABC an interview on the grounds of Camp David, a presidential preserve that remained resolutely out of range for newsmen in the Nixon years.

Left: ABC technicians hook up Ford and interviewer Harry Reasoner with special wireless microphones. The transmitting unit for the mike, which is hooked onto the shirt, goes in the hip pocket. Naval Aide Todd watches the proceedings, as does television adviser Robert Mead, behind Ford. In the background, between the men, is photographer Kennerly. The other men are security agents. Right: The two principals walk along one of the paved roads from the helicopter pad to Aspen Lodge, Ford's quarters at Camp David. The retreat is on top of the Catoctin Mountains, about sixty miles north of Washington. When Franklin Roosevelt used it, the place was called Shangri-la. Dwight Eisenhower named it after his grandson, David, who later married Julie Nixon. Nixon used Camp David more than any modern President, sometimes spending days in solitude contemplating big decisions. For Ford, Camp David is more of an athletic base, where he can stretch his legs, play tennis and swim.

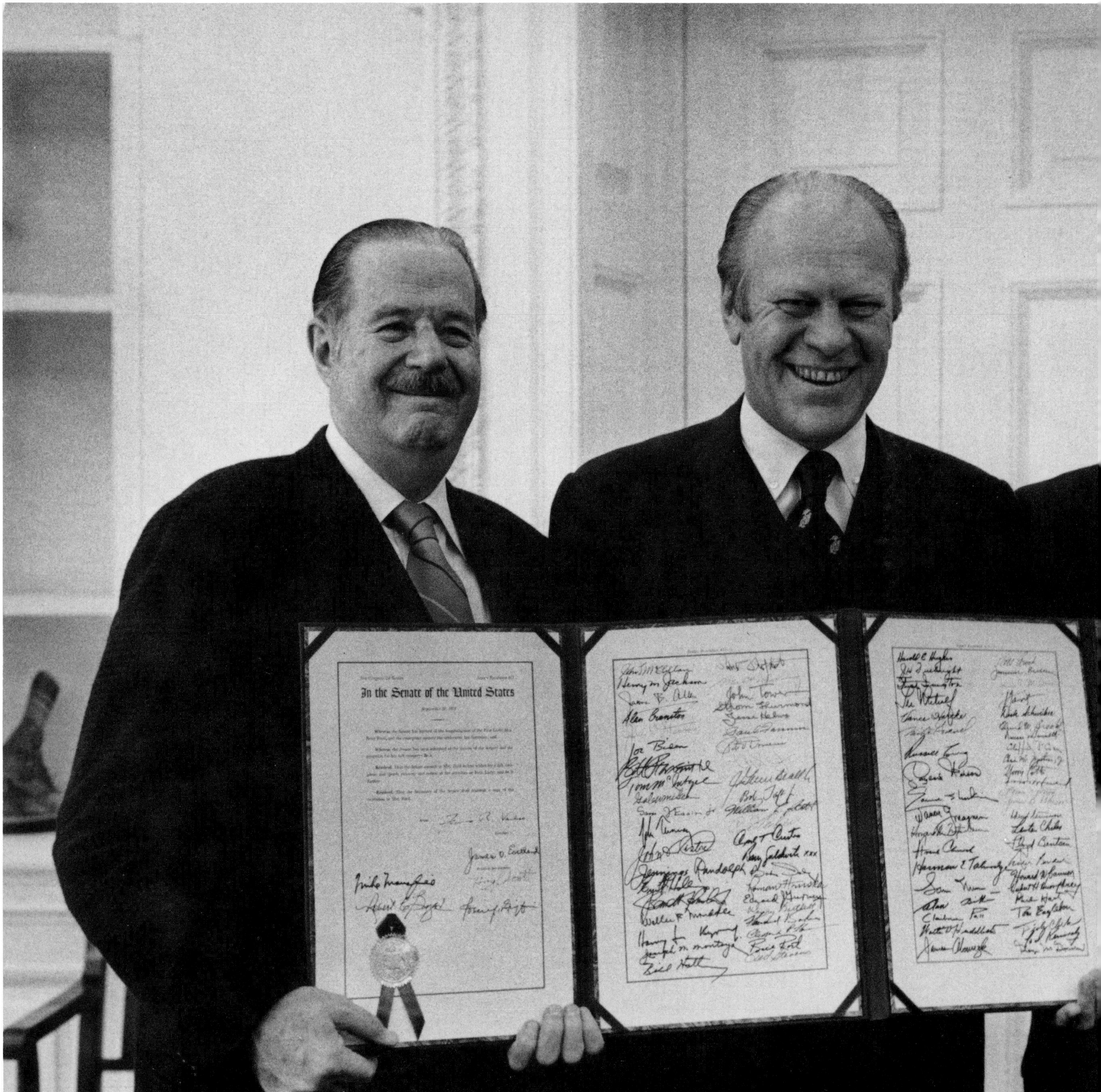
In the Senate of the United States

Where the time goes. The ceremonial burden carried by the President is heavy—too heavy, many people think. He is asked to make thousands of speeches, to honor visiting dignitaries and listen to high school bands. Each congressman and senator has some special cause that he wants the President to endorse. The requests in recent years have not diminished, but grown. And with Ford, an open man with a great many personal and professional friends, the time spent in these genial rituals became a cause of concern. Here he is shown with two old friends, Senate Minority Leader Hugh Scott, left, and Majority Leader Mike Mansfield, right. They hold the United States Senate version of a get-well card. It is a declaration wishing Mrs. Ford a speedy recovery from her cancer operation and it was signed by all one hundred members of the Senate. Scott and Mansfield delivered the document with appropriate speeches, then of course the President insisted that they pose for White House photographer Kennerly so that they could be sent a picture of the event. The gracious Ford felt he had to make some gesture in return. He rummaged around the Oval Office and came up with some tobacco that had been sent to him as a gift and gave this to his two visitors, both pipe smokers, as a token of his appreciation. It was a warm moment in Ford's October 2. But as it does in all such interludes, the clock ticked on and the President's day grew shorter— though not the list of those who wanted some of his time.

Even the President found this routine to be tedious. For a hundred of his precious minutes Ford sat in a chair in the Oval Office while 135 nonincumbent Republican congressional candidates were paraded in, each one granted half a minute. The purpose was to take still pictures and movies of the moment with the President, which the candidates could use in their campaigns. The photographic lights were set up in the President's office and the candidates lined up outside the door. The line was so long that it went down the hall, through the Cabinet Room and out into the Rose Garden. A man from the Republican Congressional Campaign Committee, which had arranged the mass endorsement, held a stopwatch to be sure each person was limited to thirty seconds of presidential time. When each candidate was at the door of the office, he or she handed a name card to an aide. The name was recorded, the person introduced to Ford, the cameras started rolling. Ford asked where each came from, the pros-

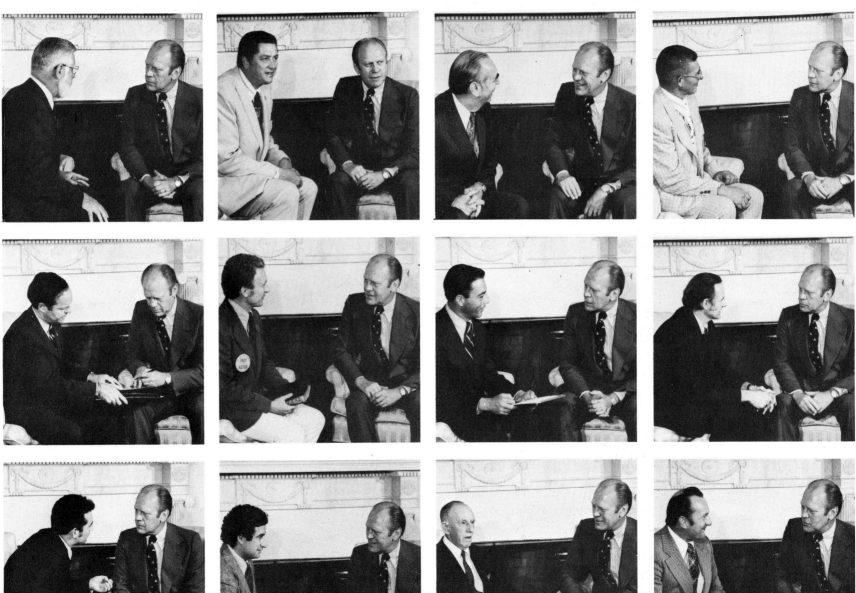

pects of victory. By the end of an hour and a half the President was plainly tired of this duty and later in the day he told his aides that too much time had been consumed. Some students of the presidency believe that the time has come to halt such incursions on presidential time, perhaps to designate a full-time ceremonial assistant or Vice-President.

Top: Ford yuks it up at what became known around the White House as the "laugh hour." To try to consolidate quirky congressional appeals for the President's time, Ford set aside one hour a month in which he honored almost any request from any congressman for any purpose. They came by the dozens, bearing gifts, dragging along friends. In this picture Congressman John Hunt, right, and three Masons from the Crescent Temple, Trenton, New Jersey, have just presented Ford with two hand-carved pipes. Below, left: Mrs. Lew Walts, the wife of the executive vice-president of the National Turkey Federation, gets a presidential handshake in return for the turkey given to Ford for the White House Thanksgiving. The turkey appears to be less enthusiastic. One of its colleagues, neatly frozen, was also presented to Ford. Below, right: The President takes a ceremonial dig at the dedication of the LBJ Memorial Grove along the Potomac River. Lady Bird Johnson looks on. Far right: Ford contemplates, with a notable lapse of ebullience, another trophy from another day—an apple presented to him by Miss Judy Miller, the 1974 Michigan Apple Queen.

When terHorst, who had covered Ford in Grand Rapids, moved into the press secretary's job, the White House press corps immediately christened the four men "the Grand Rapids Mafia."

Ford as President of the United States continued to wear funny hats, welcome the Shriners and go to prayer breakfasts, and invoked the name of God whenever he got a chance. He kept track of the big sports figures and of course the news about the University of Michigan was high on his interest list. Only a few minutes after landing in Vladivostok for his summit meeting with Leonid Brezhnev Ford spied reporter Peter Lisagor, another Michigan alumnus, in the press corps. "Hey, Pete," he called, "what's the score at half time?" He was asking about the Ohio State–Michigan game that weekend. Ford had crossed the international date line and was a day ahead of himself. The game had not started. But when it did, the Air Force had arranged to have the results. The morning after his long negotiations with Brezhnev, Ford was out of bed at 7:10 a.m. and the first news he got from his military aide, Major Robert Barrett, was that Ohio State had beaten Michigan 12-10. Ford was chagrined. He wanted more information on the game, and when he was told Michigan had outplayed Ohio State, he expressed his disappointment. It lingered throughout the summit. On the train going back to the airport after announcing the new nuclear arms agreement, Ford rehashed the game again, even in the general euphoria of successful summitry, lamenting that the field goal kicker had failed Michigan two years in a row.

The President's rhetoric is that of respectable people from an age when they talked to each other whether they had anything to say or not. He showered down his appreciation for any gestures made along his new,

kingly route—and there were many. "Thank you very much" sometimes was changed to "Thank you very, very much." His curiosity was genuine and with his powerful companions he seemed to make up in sincerity what he lacked in flair. "How much snow do you get in Moscow?" he asked Brezhnev. And when he got to the meeting site near Vladivostok, Ford inquired, "Is this a beautiful rest camp in summertime?"

The President continued to smoke Sir Walter Raleigh in his pipe or just about anything else that was handy. He ate cottage cheese for lunch and kept his English muffin routine for breakfast, although he quickly got the idea that there was someone else around to toast the muffins.

He wore the clothes that he had been wearing as Vice-President, sometimes loud plaid coats or trousers and button-down shirt collars. Often his jacket hung open and he worked in shirt sleeves if he felt like it. He was a Ford, not a Lincoln, he told the nation, and he did his best to carry out the image. Sitting around with his principal aides, Ford decreed that the central part of the White House would no longer be called "the mansion" but would be known as "the residence." He banished the royal "we" from the presidential vocabulary and so instructed his speechwriters. He ordered that the Army's Silver Trumpets, which had often heralded the approach of the President, were to be cut out of most ceremonies. The playing of "Hail to the Chief" was to be limited. Jerry Ford wanted to continue to be Jerry Ford. "Mr. President," intoned one of his old friends, U.S. Steel's William Whyte, talking over the phone one evening. "Yes, Mr. Whyte," came back the answer. Some writers felt it more natural to continue using Jerry instead of Gerald in print.

The common touch so desired by Ford is not trivial in the game of presidential leadership. When the small nerve ends of everyday experience begin to go dead in the Oval Office, then the illusions of invinci-

Ford's morning routine usually starts about 6 a.m. with a few minutes of exercise on his bicycles and with his weights in his private study. Then he showers and, without tie and jacket, goes across the sitting room to the family dining room. On most mornings Mrs. Ford is not up and Ford breakfasts alone on orange juice, melon, English muffins and tea with lemon. A small Sony color television set is placed on the table in front of Ford so he can watch a morning news show. On a table brought up beside the President's chair, he spreads out his Washington Post and New York Times. Ford's breakfast hour is almost always a time of study of the news. He scans both papers thoroughly before going back to his room to put on his tie and jacket and head for the office. Like Nixon, Ford gets a news summary. But unlike Nixon, who did not read much in the papers, Ford spends as much time as necessary on getting a complete feel of what is printed each morning.

bility and grandeur set in. Ford had seen it happen to Lyndon Johnson and Richard Nixon. His campaign for humility was deliberate.

If he had a hero among modern Presidents it was probably Harry Truman, whose great strength was his ability to identify with the man in the street. Truman never forgot who he was and where he came from. One of the first touches Ford gave his new offices after he became President was to hang a portrait of Harry Truman in the Cabinet Room. And when he was off in Asia and Mrs. Ford redecorated the Oval Office, she put a bust of Truman, with one of Lincoln, along the wall. Harry Truman, the epitome of guts and plain talk, was to be just a few steps from Ford's left hand when he was at the desk, as if Ford wanted the crusty old warrior to be part of the new Republican spirit.

In those first months of his stewardship, Ford went up to the Hill dozens of times to go through the familiar rituals of friendship, to squeeze an arm or two, to savor the musty scent of the back offices with his friends. He had the leaders of the parties down for breakfast, for dinner, for drinks. For a time there was fear that the congressmen would overwhelm the executive office in their zeal to get a little of the presidential star dust. Ford stood for almost three hours one day to be photographed with all the Republican candidates for reelection. And at Christmas the White House bash for all of Congress and their wives and husbands was one of the warmest and gayest in memory. It was plain that Jerry Ford would continue to be a man from the Hill, even to the point where it might cause him a good bit of trouble.

His other contacts in the nation and especially around Washington ran to Republican establishment figures like Melvin Laird and Bryce Harlow, who had been in and out of the Nixon administration. Ford continued to be a regular at Burning Tree Golf Club, the males-only preserve of Wash-

ington's power structure. There he hobnobbed with corporate types such as Whyte and Rodney Markley, a vice-president of the Ford Motor Company. It was not unnatural that a man of Ford's political lineage should know powerful industrial figures. His orientation and his political roots linked him to the productive machinery of the nation. As far as anybody knew, Ford's relationships with these men were honorable and open. But because of the corrupt campaign practices of the Nixon administration, what had always been a vigorous and sometimes even helpful relationship between business and government was instantly suspect. Any President sooner or later comes to realize that this nation's power rests on its industrial prowess. "It makes the mare go," said Lyndon Johnson. That corporate America should have a big voice in government is not only right but necessary. As in so many things, Nixon and his henchmen abandoned open debate for the backroom deal with shady characters who were looking for a quick fix or a way to circumvent the law. The legacy was another Nixon obstacle that Gerald Ford had to overcome.

Slowly but perceptibly Ford's manner began to flavor the White House. I noted the contrast. The few times that I was allowed into the back corridors of the White House during the Nixon years, the atmosphere was repressive—one of fear. Secretaries and those young, eager aides were never certain just how to treat one of the enemy, as most reporters were officially designated. They avoided contact, went out of their way not to encounter the newsmen as they hurried through the ordered and soundless halls. It was like being in a correctional institution. On my first pilgrimage into the sanctums of Ford, there was genial confusion. A couple of congressmen meandered down the hall arguing about Ford's economic program. White House aides called to one another and waved. I was given several handshakes and made to feel welcome. Once again there was the feeling that the business being done in those premises was everybody's business.

The Shortest Honeymoon

The honeymoon ended abruptly at 11:05, September 8, 1974. In pardoning Richard Nixon of all Watergate crimes known and unknown, Gerald Ford suffered an instant twenty-two-point decline in national affection and, many thought, did untold damage to the fragile sense of commitment to what is right.

The early chapters of this extraordinary event are still less than clear, and though Ford would explain it over and over, even going to the unusual length of testifying personally before a congressional committee, he could not in his first months dispel the doubts his action had raised about his political and ethical judgment.

The pardon came at a curious time — a Sunday morning. Hasty calls went out all over Washington, rounding up the sleepy reporters who had not already left for the country or the tennis courts. They shuffled into the President's office fully expecting that Ford would be making some announcement on the economy or foreign policy. While some felt it would be important, others were skeptical, wondering if the new Ford administration was not possibly overselling the news it was about to make.

Ford strode into the Oval Office with his mouth set. He was, everyone agreed, unusually somber. He wore a dark suit and a white shirt that he had put on for church. He carried with him a manila folder, which he placed on his clean, polished desk. On the desktop there was a single pen, a clue that some decree had to be signed by the President. There was no banter with the small group of reporters, another hint that, at least to Ford, the matter was extremely serious. He looked up at the camera crew in front of him and asked, "Are you all set?" They nodded, and Ford began to read.

"I have come to a decision which I felt I should tell you, and all my fellow citizens, as soon as I was certain in my own mind and conscience that it is the right thing to do. . . ."

When he had finished, Ford picked up the felt-tip pen, and with his lips pursed he signed his name to the "full, free, and absolute" pardon of Richard M. Nixon. He rose silently, turned and walked resolutely from the office. There was no turning back.

In moments like this, when a President has made a tough call, his staff instantly rallies to buck him up. They did in those few seconds after Ford signed the decree. Oddly, some of the men congratulated Ford, one of those reflexes of an aide to almost any presidential action. It was, perhaps, not really a time for congratulations. He may have sensed the doubt in that moment. "Well," he said, "I think it was the right thing to do."

The President then went on out for a round of golf with Melvin Laird at Burning Tree, a place about as far removed from the realities of the Oval Office as can be found in Washington.

The rest of the nation got the news as slowly as they usually do on a Sunday. But by late afternoon there was little doubt about the fury of the response. People like West Virginia's Senator Robert Byrd, a growing power in Congress, expressed shock and disappointment. "I think this sets a double standard," Byrd said. "It will reopen a lot of old sores," declared Peter Rodino, the chairman of the House Judiciary Committee, which had conducted the impeachment inquiry. "Without a declaration of personal guilt from Nixon, the whole thing is still up in the air," said Chesterfield Smith, a former president of the American Bar Association. "My whole position on Watergate has been to get to the truth," historian James MacGregor Burns said. "To the extent that the pardon interferes with that process, it is most unfortunate."

There were a few voices raised in support. But, for the most part, they were the expected ones and thus were of little help in stemming the tide of disillusion. "It was the only decent and prudent course to follow,"

Arizona's Senator Barry Goldwater stated. Vice-President-designate Nelson Rockefeller rallied loyally, saying it was "an act of conscience, compassion and courage."

But America did not appear to think so — by a ratio of sixty-two to thirty-one, according to pollster George Gallup. What was surprising was the vehemence of the public protest. For the first time Ford was jeered and picketed in his public appearances. Outside his hotel in Pittsburgh the people waved signs ("The Country Won't Stand for It"), and in Pinehurst, North Carolina, where the President had gone for the pleasant assignment of dedicating the World Golf Hall of Fame, more protestors showed up ("Is Nixon Above the Law?"). In college debate and from church pulpits Ford's decision was denounced. It was a peculiar time in which traditional political loyalties were seemingly reversed. Conservatives seemed to be the most outraged at the pardon, liberals more resigned and ready to move on to confront the nation's other problems.

From San Clemente there was silence at first, then expressions of gratitude, then reports that Richard Nixon was in a state of physical exhaustion and emotional depression. Somehow Nixon and the men who had gone into exile with him still searched for the miracle — as they had all through the Watergate case — that would overnight dispel the charges against the former President and lift the burden of his personal guilt. The storm against Ford's pardon deepened the ex-President's despair.

After years of government by conspiracy it was hard for almost anyone to get rid of the notion that here was yet another blow, that Gerald Ford had made a deal when he was Vice-President, that he was no better than the other schemers who had been forced out of office. Ford's unaccustomed secrecy in arriving at his decision fueled the rumors. His thoughts about pardoning Nixon had been aired with only his closest aides.

Never before in history had a President gone formally to Capitol Hill to submit to questions by a congressional committee. Ford did it on October 17 to try to explain his reasons for pardoning Richard Nixon. For days the move had been debated in the White House. Some of the President's aides feared it was an unhealthy precedent, a step that would lead to more demands by more committees. Ford brushed aside the objections and appeared alone at the witness table. For two hours he answered questions after delivering a lengthy statement detailing how the pardon was conceived and carried out. The episode had been precipitated when Congressman William Hungate's subcommittee of the Judiciary Committee submitted written questions to Ford to answer. When Ford decided to make the unusual gesture of appearing in person, the full committee assembled, with Hungate presiding, Committee Chairman Peter Rodino off to the side (sixth from the left). Though, as always in these matters, new questions were raised almost as soon as Ford answered the old ones, the gesture by the President created such a favorable feeling in Congress that the controversy over the pardon began to subside slowly.

Even Buchen and speechwriter Robert Hartmann warned of the consequences of a pardon, noting a poll which showed that 56 percent of the public thought Nixon should be tried. "I don't need to read the polls to tell me whether I'm right or not," Ford grumped.

As part of the pardon, Ford devised an intricate deal on the presidential tapes. In a series of cross-continental flights, a young lawyer named Benton L. Becker worked out an agreement for court access to the tapes for five years, but after that point Nixon was to have the right to order them destroyed. Ford studied its final details the day before he gave the pardon and sent Hartmann and Buchen off to write his statement. On the day of the pardon Ford went across Lafayette Park to church at Saint John's, then hurried back to his office to go over the statement. He read the speech aloud twice to Hartmann, making a few minor changes and adding his concern about Nixon's health to the reasons for granting the pardon. As the hour approached, Ford began to phone the people he thought should have advance warning. He had not consulted with anyone outside his small coterie — not Special Procescutor Leon Jaworski, who had immense interest in gaining access to the tapes; nor Attorney General William Saxbe; not even congressional leaders. Those he phoned now he did not ask for advice; he told them what he was going to do. House Majority Leader Thomas ("Tip") O'Neill, Jr., with whom Ford often golfed, was stunned. "Jesus," he told Ford. "Don't you think it's kind of early?" Ford's mind was set firmly.

I watched the final acts of the Nixon presidency from both inside and outside Washington. While I was somewhat of the same mind as Ford, that we should put Nixon behind us and get on with the nation's business, I was constantly reminded in my travels of how pervasive and bitter the feeling against Nixon was in most parts of the country. It was a particular irony for me, because I had been one of those convinced from the start that Nixon had both ordered the Watergate break-in and then directed the cover-up, and for two years both in lectures and in writing I had said so. (It remains my conviction today, although only half of the accusation is yet proved.) Most Americans, however, responded rather slowly to the events. Their faith gradually eroded as the evidence against Nixon was painfully being gathered. But they were reluctant to draw too many conclusions. They simply did not want to believe that a President was guilty of such crimes, and even near the end there was a sizable group who held to their suspicions that the crime was more a product of the press than of the White House. What I and many others did not anticipate was that when the roof finally fell in on Nixon, those people who had clung to him for so long, even the most rational and informed, would transfer their emotional energy to their indignation and demand that he be tried and punished for his offenses.

This has always been a forgiving nation — in politics as well as in war. Somehow the intensity of the outcry against Ford's pardon of Nixon seemed almost out of character. Pondering these things one afternoon in early October, I called up Press Secretary Ron Nessen and said I would like to talk privately with the President about his reasons for giving the pardon. Next day the answer came back. Ford would see me for half an hour the following evening.

Nessen and I talked for a few minutes in his office before he walked back with me to the Oval Office. It was the first time in five years I had had a chance for this kind of interview. The simple elegance of the Cabinet Room struck me again as I walked by the door. Most of our nation's modern history had been debated in that room. In the secretary's office, where we paused for a moment, I was greeted by Nell Yates, whom I had first met when John Kennedy was President. She is one of those loyal and efficient souls who do more than we know to keep a government going from administration to administration. The door swung open and there was Ford, standing at the far end of the Oval Office behind his desk, head down, studying the papers spread out on the desktop. I had witnessed that same scene with five Presidents. They stand in the same place, snatching the few seconds it takes a visitor to walk up to their desk. They are framed in the tall windows with the bulletproof glass that look out over the South Lawn. Ford looked up. "Glad to see you," he said. "How are you?" He scooped up his pipe and pouch of tobacco and moved around his desk, shook hands, then gestured toward the couch in front of the fireplace. He half sat, half sprawled on the couch as he tamped down the tobacco, explaining, "More comfortable here." Then he talked about why he had given Richard Nixon the pardon. Whether it was, in the long run, a wise decision or not, it follows faithfully the profile of Jerry Ford.

He had been bothered, Ford said, after he had received three or four questions about a possible pardon in his first press conference in late August and had walked back to the Oval Office pondering the issue. He had told the reporters that he was going to let any judicial proceedings run their natural course. But it was clear that the questions asked that afternoon would grow and continue to plague him and to divide the attention and energy of the nation, which so desperately needed to move on to vital questions of the economy, energy and food. Every day all the papers had headlines asking about Nixon's future and about the tapes. From the beginning Ford knew that at some time he would pardon Nixon. He did not think it was in the national interest to have a former President in jail. But when? Ford began to consider the action he ultimately took on September 8. He said that he had called in Phil Buchen and asked for a study about the legal precedents of pardon. He had pondered the question of a fair trial and what would

happen if Nixon was in the dock. How long would a trial take? He had concluded that it might go on for eighteen months.

There was no historical precedent, Ford learned. It was all so new. He felt after his talk with Buchen that he could give a blanket pardon, and over the next days his conviction grew that there would be only one way to really get the matter behind the nation. He was sure that there would be a national shock from the pardon but felt that its effects would vanish with time as he began to take action on other issues. Thus, step by step he had moved quietly down to the final act of signing the decree.

Ford talked easily and openly on this day. He seemed, as he always had, to be a guileless man. If what he had done was a mistake, that was for history to record. But he had done it out of conviction, not because he had made a deal.

No, Ford said in answer to a question, he had not gone back to study the actions of other Presidents to find some guidance for this situation. He had followed his own instincts. For a few minutes he talked about those. "I was never a person who thought you ought to get the last pound of flesh as a lawyer or in political life," Ford mused. "I was never vindictive that I knew about." He guessed that forgiveness was a Middle Western trait that he had acquired years ago. In the pardon he saw some elements of the techniques he had used on the Hill. He had always felt "you had to give a little to get a little." This was, in a way, what he had done with Nixon. To separate the Watergate issue from his presidency, Ford had taken an action that in other circumstances he might not have. But it was a way of resolving a greater problem for the country. "Holding a grudge a long time doesn't make much sense," said Ford. "It is not my nature."

The President shifted his long frame on the couch, fiddled with his pipe, smiled at the troubles that his action had stirred. Yes, he said, it had been beyond anything he had reckoned. But, Ford continued, he thought people were even then beginning to perceive the wisdom of the act. He had just read the sermon given by Duncan Littlefair, the Grand Rapids pastor, which supported him. After all, he pointed out, he and Duncan Littlefair had been genial political opposites for twenty-six years.

There had been no deal, Ford reiterated. In the hours before Nixon stepped down, all kinds of proposals had been made. Nixon's men had talked to Ford and he had turned their suggestions aside. What about the tapes? "I felt caught in the middle," he said. "What do you do with the documents and tapes? I wanted to get them away from me. I didn't want to be caught in a court fight so every time there was a question they would turn to me for an answer."

Ford talked about his view of Nixon during the last hours. It was preposterous, he said, to believe that Nixon was somehow escaping from guilt. Nixon was a tragic figure, who had been destroyed inside by Watergate. Ford had watched him those last months and weeks, he said. As minority leader he had gone to the White House for meetings and had seen how Nixon had trouble keeping his mind on the subjects under discussion. "He just wasn't the same strong person that I knew who had fought up and down the Hill all those years, a man who had taken the bitter with the sweet and always been able to go on," said Ford.

In all those other battles, said Ford, Nixon had never really changed. But in Watergate he had. On that last day when he had been summoned by Nixon, Ford had studied the man closely as they talked about the presidency, the nation and the world for more than an hour. "I noticed he had grayed considerably," Ford said. "He was drawn — his collar didn't fit the way it used to. He could talk about the subjects all right. He could pull himself together. But I noticed that

it took a lot of effort. He was drawing upon his reserves."

I got the impression as I listened that compassion for a doomed man might have been more in Ford's mind than he had told the public. Though Ford did not say it, there certainly were overtones in his conversation that suggested he was wondering if Nixon would live very long.

In the end, although the process of pardon was extremely complicated (as most presidential actions have become), it rested upon the simple convictions of a plain person that the nation needed to put Watergate behind it and that a sick and burdened man needed now to be left alone.

Our time was up, though Ford seemed a bit reluctant to end the short interlude away from his routine. Ron Nessen, the new press secretary, who had taken the job after terHorst resigned in objection to the pardon, dozed quietly in the Kennedy rocker between the couches. He had been working eighteen hours a day. As I leaned forward to get out of the couch, Ford said that he had talked on the phone to Nixon after granting the pardon. "He called and he said, 'I'm damned sorry to have caused you all the trouble.' He said he would send the pardon back if it would help." Ford smiled, knowing that Nixon was simply showing his concern for Ford's dilemma. "I said, 'I've made the decision. You stand firm. It will work out okay.' "

As we walked toward the office door, Ford suddenly asked me if I had heard how Mrs. Nixon was faring. "Betty tried to call a couple of times and they were never able to reach Pat, she was gone or something. Have there been any pictures?" I couldn't answer the President's question, but that sudden query about Pat Nixon seemed to underscore the sincerity of the talk we had just had. There were three handshakes before I got out the door, a cheery invitation to come on back sometime, and then the Presi-

A Vice-President to be. Nelson Rockefeller, at the side of the President's desk, discusses his problems with his Senate confirmation. Ford told Rockefeller he needed his help as soon as he could possibly get it.

dent returned to that desk at the far end of the Oval Office.

Perhaps the national reaction to the Nixon pardon was so severe because the nation so much wanted to believe that Gerald Ford would solve their problems, put credibility back into leadership and ride through their midst like a man on a white horse. From the moment that Ford became President, the expectations were too great. No man could have lived up to the hopes that grew wildly in the wake of Nixon's departure. So when Ford's human dimensions became so starkly visible at the time of the pardon, the disappointment was magnified.

There was also a Watergate hangover. After viewing the widespread duplicity and criminality in the White House, the public was almost bound to suspect any action by a new President that departed from tradition. In that atmosphere the tiniest flaws were blown out of proportion. The Nixon pardon spread doubt like wildfire. Disappointment bred skepticism, which in some instances turned into ridicule. In the process of readjusting their view of Ford, many people in renewed alarm began to see the size of the problems that had been obscured by Watergate. They were suddenly Ford's problems and he was an unelected President of questionable talent.

In arriving at the selection of his vice-presidential designee, Ford had proceeded by elemental logic, yet when problems arising from Nelson Rockefeller's generosity began to cloud the nomination, they in turn fueled more doubts about Ford. It was part of the poisonous Washington atmosphere that lingered after Watergate.

Ford had collected the recommendations for Vice-President from his congressional leaders, from his friends and staff. And he had dutifully gone through the routine of weighing the men according to experience, age,

ability, political tone, acceptance in the nation and the world. But almost from the start, Rockefeller led the pack. His life had been devoted to public service. He knew Washington and he had been Governor of New York for fourteen years. Almost every major issue confronting the United States in the last thirty years had been studied by Rockefeller or by one of the commissions that the family foundation had launched. Rocky was noted for bringing the best talent needed to any problem, then listening and even hearing what the men had to say. His tough defense posture fit with Ford's own notion that the world was not yet so safe a place that we could reduce our arms unilaterally. His liberal social ideas were a bit beyond what Ford had supported, but such things could always be adjusted in a relationship as structured and top-heavy as that between President and Vice-President. There was almost no surprise when in low key Ford brought Rockefeller into the Oval Office and announced that he was the choice. Then came the news of Rockefeller's unbounded largesse to those who had served him over the years, some of the gifts coming perilously close to manifesting a conflict of interest. There had been a $50,000 gift for Henry Kissinger when he left Rockefeller's staff to join Richard Nixon's White House. William J. Ronan, the brilliant transportation expert, had received $625,000 in canceled loans and gifts out of gratitude for his services and counsel. L. Judson Morhouse, who served eight years as New York Republican chairman and was then convicted of bribery in a liquor license scandal, had a loan of $86,313 wiped off the books. So it went. In the tedious hearings that followed these revelations, there was no evidence of criminality or even intention to gain political advantage. But as the picture of the immense Rockefeller family wealth began to emerge, that, too, encouraged the idea that Ford was a President who acted too hastily, a man who had not yet put together a White House staff that could competently check out personnel or handle these unexpected crises.

At least in the case of the staff, the doubts were legitimate. Ford had acted once again with caution and compassion—and with common sense. He retained Nixon's chief of staff, Alexander Haig, simply because Haig knew how things ran in the back of the White House. But, to many, Haig was a particularly odious symbol of the Nixon days, a former general who had publicly insisted on Nixon's innocence when almost everybody else knew better. In the end, Haig had helped to ease Nixon out of office, but in this time of doubt that was largely forgotten. Other Nixon aides, such as Dean Burch and Lawrence Higby (who once was called Haldeman's Haldeman), lingered on the payroll. America was impatient for change that did not seem to be coming.

Meanwhile, Ford had discovered the joys of Air Force One and was junketing around the country trying to bring help to the dispirited Republican congressional contenders. For a time it seemed as if Ford did not perceive that among the many hats he had to wear as President, one was that of organizer and administrator, the unglamorous but essential work of getting good people to make the machinery run the way he wanted it to run.

Deepening Ford's difficulties at every turn in this period was the troubled economy. Inflation roared along at 12 percent, the dreaded "double digit." Consumer confidence began to wane, particularly in the automobile industry, and sales dropped by as much as 20 to 40 percent. The housing industry, with starts down as much as 50 percent, teetered on the brink of disaster. And cattle prices were so low that farmers began to destroy young calves rather than feed them and then sell them at yet higher losses. Even in the middle of this despair, however,

The Economic Policy Board waits for the President in the Cabinet Room. The photograph was taken by Fred Ward at the President's chair. At the right is Ford's personalized folder with the agenda and the necessary background data. In front of each chair is a blank pad for notes and a mechanical pencil, plus a silver ashtray. It is unofficial protocol for such meetings with the President that the participants wait in the chairs along the wall of the room until the President enters. Then they come forward and take their places at the huge elliptical table. The men, left to right, are Kenneth Rush, chairman of the board; Paul McCracken, former chairman of the Council of Economic Advisers; Stephen Gardner, Deputy Secretary of Treasury; James Lynn, then Secretary of Housing and Urban Development; Arthur Burns, chairman of the Federal Reserve System; Roy Ash, head of the Office of Management and Budget; and Alan Greenspan, chairman of the Council of Economic Advisers.

there were industries with soaring profits. The oil companies turned in new records and so did the steel industry. Paper makers chalked up gains, and when the sugar shortage forced prices up, one sugar firm showed a 3000 percent increase in its profit margin in one quarter. While inflation generally signals a full employment economy, unemployment mounted, and by December 1974 it had reached 6.5 percent, a level Ford acknowledged was serious. The mixture of boom and bust in industry, the onerous tangle of inflation and recession confounded even the experts. But it was all Gerald Ford's to deal with. Congress and industry and even the press simply viewed it with alarm and reported the confused opinion from the experts.

In his first address to Congress, Ford had called for a series of economic meetings around the nation to culminate in a summit session in Washington, the results of which would be employed by the White House for guidance in prescribing fresh economic potions.

By and large, the regional meetings were a success, bringing together businessmen, labor leaders, academicians, politicians who were familiar with each region's special problems. Then in October some eight hundred of these delegates assembled in the Washington Hilton Hotel for the grand finale. For the President it was a critical time. And once again he was battered by fate. Just before Ford was to appear at the meeting, his wife went to Bethesda Naval Hospital for the removal of a cancerous right breast. Less than an hour after she had come out of surgery, Ford stood somberly before the delegates and declared he was there to start the battle to rescue the economy. "You have done your work well," he told the men and women. "Now it is my turn." He sketched his ideas in a vigorous thirty-two-minute speech. It was a declaration of war, primarily on inflation and waste; the signs of the recession were not yet clear enough to influence Ford's thinking. There was no consensus in the meeting, no clear directions had emerged in the debate. But the economic summit was good. It was an educational device showing the nation the tremendous complexity of the problem.

For a week Ford and his experts pondered the advice and sorted out their moves. Then Ford went back to the Hill to appear before a joint session of Congress and announce his program. Sporting a WIN ("Whip Inflation Now") button on his lapel, he laid out the general guidelines for a 5 percent income tax surcharge on high incomes, tax relief for lower incomes, more investment credit for industry. He urged modest expansion in public service programs for the unemployed, federal help in the mortgage market and voluntary programs of fuel and food conservation. It was a nudge beyond the old Nixon nostrums, but not a big one. While nobody doubted Ford's sincerity, there was the feeling of a man trying to put together a package that would not upset too many people. The solution of the problem seemed almost secondary. It was the classic congressional response. Even as Ford spoke in the stilled House chamber there was evidence that more serious remedies would be needed before long. The world was going faster than the White House. Many powerful men of both parties instantly and openly expressed their disappointment in the Ford proposals. It was a curious time. While there seemed to be a great desire both in the nation and in Congress for sacrifice to confront the economic dilemma, Ford's requests for voluntary reductions in consumption and for an increase in taxes on the well-to-do were scorned. It seemed to be a time for all or nothing.

As many predicted, the economy continued to drift more deeply into trouble. Ford could not outrun it. That was never better illustrated than when the

There is no calculation of how much of the nation's business is transacted, how many ideas sparked, in such chance encounters as this one between Secretary of the Treasury William Simon, right, and Arthur Burns, of the Federal Reserve. The two men stand in thoughtful conversation in the Cabinet Room between sessions with the President and meetings with each other. In these moments quiet misgivings can be voiced, personal convictions expressed that oftentimes are buried in the formal meetings.

President went to Japan and Korea in November. The visits were largely ceremonial and almost every day Ford's festive tour collided on the front pages of the American press and on television with devastating new facts about the economy. On one day, as Ford hoisted his glasses of champagne in Japan, the jittery stock market slid twenty-seven points. The pictures of Ford with chalk-faced geisha girls at the Tsuruya restaurant in Kyoto ended up on the front pages just as Chrysler Corporation announced that it was closing five plants. Ford, who had committed himself to the Asian journey to show his desire to continue the foreign policy of Nixon, could do little but walk on through the routines, listening to the speeches, trying chopsticks ("I wanted to show off for the press"). The feeling that Ford should have been back home at his desk was not dispelled even when he went to Vladivostok for the meeting with Brezhnev.

But Ford got the message. Back home, he buckled down to work, spent hours in his office with his energy advisers and economic team. He did something else. Seeing more clearly than ever that he was a man woefully unprepared for the job ahead of him, Ford embarked on a crash course of remedial learning.

He jetted to New York to pick the brains of members of Nelson Rockefeller's Commission on Critical Choices. He listened to nuclear physicist Edward Teller, former Pentagon research chief John Foster. At the White House he reinstituted something John Kennedy had tried—small dinners and luncheons for scholars and ranking pundits. He sat by the hour absorbing their collected wisdom. Historian Daniel Boorstin came by; so did James Q. Wilson, a Harvard government professor; and Martin Diamond, a Woodrow Wilson Fellow at the Smithsonian; and John Robson, a Chicago lawyer. Thinkers Irving Kristol and Herman Kahn were summoned, as were journalists and commentators James Reston, Howard K. Smith, John Osborne, Charles Bartlett and David Broder. To keep the idea pipeline open, Ford appointed Robert A. Goldwin, a former Guggenheim fellow, as a liaison with the academic community.

One of the intellectual visitors came away from the White House with new hope that Ford was reaching beyond himself. It was not unlike Thomas Jefferson's evenings of conversations with the accomplished men of his time, an enlightened procedure that left the country poorer when it declined. While the men who called on Ford did not emerge with the idea that he was ever going to be a powerhouse, they were impressed with his awareness of the problems facing the United States and his desire for historical and philosophical perspective. The press posed the question hopefully in those days: Was this the real beginning of the education of President Gerald Ford?

Politics and Diplomacy

A wet end to a joyful excursion below the border. Here, Ford waves to the crowd at Tucson, Arizona, in the farewell ceremonies for Mexican President Luis Echeverría Alvarez. Earlier the two Presidents had started their get-acquainted journey in Mexico, to the cheers of villagers who lined the streets along their route. Then they took helicopters to the U.S. side for a press conference and a view of an American crowd. For politicians of any country and persuasion, the enthusiasm of people acts like a stimulant, bringing smiles to the leaders despite their many problems.

In our time the rituals of domestic politics have become so important that they have sometimes replaced the meaning, and the goals of improving and guiding society have drowned in the joy of possessing and parading power. Motion, appearance, balloons, hoopla and boozy dinners, only footnotes in our true political heritage, became almost ends in themselves. Never was the game more of a mechanical miracle than in the presidency of Richard Nixon, where television, jets, canned speeches, planned demonstrations, brass bands and pretty girls were flawlessly meshed with the gears of the White House machinery. What was said hardly mattered. What was meant—well, who knew? Or cared? It was all show biz.

For several decades there had been an evolution in campaign styles paralleling America's advances in technology and communication. Lyndon Johnson was credited with first using a helicopter effectively in his run for the Senate from Texas in 1948. Dwight Eisenhower first used television extensively; John Kennedy defined and enlarged the idea. Once in the White House, Kennedy grew so fond of his Boeing 707 as a political instrument that he invented the twenty-hour campaign day. He traveled with the sun across America, then flew back to Washington comfortably asleep in his airborne bed. At times, when they arrived a little earlier than anticipated, the pilot would park Air Force One in a quiet corner of the ramp and let Kennedy finish his rest.

What Presidents did was of course emulated by other pols to the degree that money would permit. When Gerald Ford was minority leader he jetted as much as two hundred thousand miles a year, speaking for Republicans, raising money, swept along by some inner compulsion that no politician can really explain. He was

away from home as many as two hundred nights a year, eating bad food, shaking hands, making forgettable speeches, but moving, happily moving across the vast electronic stage. If there was an enduring declaration by Ford in all that time, it has been covered over by events. But his political habits were hardened. Archaic rites are expanded to furious proportions with modern machines.

Certainly there must be some benefit to a congressional candidate who shows his voters that he knows and is beloved by the powerful men of Washington. Such pilgrimages as those made by Ford in his congressional days probably build a camaraderie in the party structure, which is valuable back in Congress. But basically, the campaign system is outdated. Torchlight parades, ancient ancestors of the jet caravan, had a certain social significance. People did not get together that often seventy-five years ago. And there was substance. It was the only chance a voter had to see and hear a candidate. Outrageous claims by the candidates of their virtues and abilities were made then, too, but were quietly discounted by the audiences, who simply wanted to be there and take the fellow's measure in person. Television has cut the necessity for frantic movement, notably in presidential campaigning. The level of education in the United States, the degree of awareness of most of the population, have made candor and simplicity more appealing. Yet many Washington politicians now travel more and speak more nonsense than ever.

It is unthinking habit. Innovation in politics lags behind progress in almost all other human endeavors. In October of 1974 President Ford went on the campaign trail as he had always done. The presidency magnified his voice and his reach, but it did not basically alter his perceptions.

In the months before the 1974 midterm election he traveled 16,685 miles, giving eighty-five speeches in twenty states, shaking an estimated 16,000 hands, being seen and heard by nearly 900,000 people and beamed over television to uncounted millions more.

When the gleaming blue and silver presidential jet swooped out of the sky, some small communities were literally paralyzed. Children were dismissed from schools, businesses were closed, roads blocked off, and the citizens were exhorted to go to the airport or come down to the civic auditorium for the big rally.

Ford was an eager and easy man who launched into his dubious political effort like a missionary out to save the heathen. The task was formidable. With Watergate still a live issue, the pardon of Nixon fresh in everyone's mind, the American public were turned off Republicans as they had not been for forty years. Democrat Tip O'Neill, House majority leader, warned his old friend when he golfed with him at Burning Tree. "It's going to be an avalanche," he said. O'Neill's private prediction was that his party would gain from forty to sixty seats in the House.

Whether or not he admitted it, Ford had been campaigning almost since he had stepped into the Oval Office. It is instinctive in the congressional breed in an election year. Their metabolism attunes their behavior to the November confrontation. At first the Nixon pardon gave Ford pause because of the demonstrations he encountered. But by October there was no holding him back. His worry that there would be a Democratic avalanche was sounded at every stop. Preserve the two-party system, he urged. "I don't believe the American people want a veto-proof Congress. I believe that the Democrats, too, have realized that the American people don't want a dictatorial government and now they, too, are backing away from that idea." But the polls continued to show that the American people, and particularly the Democrats, were of an opposite mind. The Republican malaise deepened.

In Philadelphia Ford danced a polka with Mary Scranton, the wife of the former governor, puffed on his pipe, pumped the hands of the fat cats who had paid $150 for the privilege and the dinner. One reporter watching Ford observed that he obviously relished the routine and said in astonishment, "He even likes the food."

The miles reeled off beneath Air Force One, paid for by the Republican National Committee at $1,918 per flying hour. Michigan, Missouri, Kansas, South Dakota, Indiana, Oklahoma, Ohio. On one excursion he dipped below the Arizona border for some foreign politicking. In the little town of Magdalena, Mexico, he and Mexican President Echeverría held a get-acquainted meeting, and crowds of jubilant Mexicans filled the narrow streets, racing after the shirt-sleeved Presidents, showering confetti down on them and throwing flowers in their path. There were bands and cheers and laughter, the heady whiff of distant cultures. It was like a tonic. Ford glowed.

But the gay strains of the mariachis stilled and the cheering thinned when Ford flew back to his own ground and a rally at Oklahoma City. In the Myriad Center, with a capacity of 12,000, there were vast empty areas even though the diligent advance men had trucked in six high school bands. The people in the stands rallied some when Ford took the podium, but their enthusiasm soon died as he doled out the usual clichés against wasteful Democrats and in praise of tight-fisted Republicans, in this case Henry Bellmon ("He calls the shots as he sees them"), who was running for re-election to the Senate. So sonorous was the exhortation that most people paid little heed when Ford declared his concern that "if we get the wrong kind of Congress, peace could be in jeopardy."

That is the kind of political talk that congressmen and senators make all the time and nobody much pays attention. But when a President says it, things are different. Reporters pay attention to such details. And almost instantly, the new shot at the Democrats clattered out over the wires.

Ford droned on, oblivious to the ruckus he had just raised.

On the same day Democratic Chairman Robert Strauss was making his way to Winner, South Dakota, trying desperately to win a headline here, to get a little television time there. He was, admittedly, not having much luck, with Ford on the campaign trail and interest in Nixon still running high. Then he got word of Ford's "jeopardy" speech and flew right back to Chicago to set himself up in the rebuttal business. For the next two days Strauss was on prime time with his carefully calculated indignation, likening Ford's remarks to "Nixon-Agnew" campaign tactics, "the same kind of rhetoric and the same sort of attempt to appeal to the baser instincts of the American people."

The White House groped for an answer but the damage was done—another lesson for Ford. The casual language of congressional campaigns will not do for a President. By the time the presidential jets reached Cleveland that night, the words had been toned down. Ford did the same to the audience. He talked too long, as was his habit, and what enthusiasm he was granted at the start of the speech soon evaporated as he went into his warnings about inflation and big spending. The Republican audiences wanted something more from Ford. He could not find that something. Perhaps, after two of the worst political years in our history for any party, there was no man who could give them the combination of trust, inspiration and humor they craved. But at least Ford did not give up. Why did he do it? reporters asked Ford one night, returning from a long day of campaigning. There was not much he could do to help, and if disaster overtook the Republicans, which seemed inevitable, he would only be blamed for it. Ford conceded the grim picture. But, he told those huddled around him, if he remained holed up in the White House and massive defeat came, Republicans everywhere would say, "He didn't even try.... At least I tried." But politicians never quite believe things are as bad

as they may be. They are in the business because of some unquenchable optimism, some special reserve of confidence in their personal magnetism and inspirational qualities. That feeling flickered in Ford. He looked again at the newsmen waiting for his words, then spoke over the roar of the jet engines. "And if the results are better than the polls say..." He smiled. That is the perpetual dream for men of politics in motion.

There was a bright moment for Ford. It was back in his hometown of Grand Rapids. He badly wanted his old congressional seat to be returned to the Republicans. When he had been named Vice-President, Ford had been shocked when Democrat Richard Vanderveen won the special election. Now Vanderveen was up again and a friend of Ford's, Paul Goebel, Jr., was running on the Republican ticket. Ford gave it everything he had, and the people in Grand Rapids seemed to respond, but as it turned out the enthusiasm was for the hometown kid, Jerry Ford, not the Republicans.

A thousand or so very hardy souls made their way to the airport to see the new President land in a driving rain. Ford did not disappoint them. He emerged from the jet coatless, stood in the rain shaking every hand that was extended. They were his friends, his people. Downtown at the rally at Vandenberg Center, another fifteen thousand huddled in the wet to hear their boy drone through his down-home clichés. It didn't matter. He meant what he said and the warmth came through. "I am just overwhelmed, and words are inadequate to express everything I feel deep down in my heart.... I saw friends I went to Madison School with, friends that I went to South High with, friends that I worked with in many, many scientific projects...."

The contrasting rituals of political celebration are shown in these pictures taken within hours of each other. At the right is the view down the main street of the Mexican village of Magdalena de Kino. Ford and Echeverría walked along the street beneath the banners and the large pictures of themselves. In shirt sleeves, they were pelted with carnations and cheered every step of the way. At the end of the street they paused to pay their respects at the crypt that contained the bones

of Father Kino, the priest who served the people in the area. Later, the men were deposited by helicopter in Tubac, Arizona. Left: The American crowd around the chopper pad is blasted by the wind from the rotors, their enthusiasm undiminished despite the buffeting.

Along the campaign trail, Ford takes
the classic position of the candidate.
The raw lumber of a new speakers'
stand at Anderson, South Carolina, is
only partially disguised by the traditional bunting. The speech was given
in front of the new building of the
Anderson Independent and the Daily
Mail. Ford dedicated the structure,
talking about the importance of freedom
of the press. Behind the stand, an
ever watchful Secret Service agent
scans the scene.

There is nothing I can say except thank you, every one of you, for being here."

The rain kept coming and Jerry Ford kept talking, real stuff from inside him. Only if you were from Grand Rapids could you really understand what it meant for the President of the United States to come back home this way.

"And may I thank Althea Bennett here for the box of cookies which she has given me.... I used to stop in at Petersen's drugstore for early breakfast, and she was there to prepare it, and I used to enjoy those cookies very much then...."

He could not stop. Each new face, each view he saw before him reminded him of his past. "It was a great privilege to go to your service club, to your Farm Bureau community meeting, to go to your churches, to your city hall, to meet you on the street, to go to the Lowell Showboat, rodeo, the Red Flannel celebration. ...It is the warmth, it is the friendliness, it is the look in the eye of people that makes you welcome.... And you know the Federal Building. I used to have an office right up there in the corner. I used to look down here, and I could see at various times of the day there would be periodic meetings and wonderful luncheon gatherings. Occasionally we had a demonstration or two, and sometimes in the moonlight I could look down and see a few friendly people holding hands. And what is wrong with that?" The people on the streets of Grand Rapids drank in the words. It was the magic that Ford had been vainly trying to capture in all his political wanderings. Before he flew back to Washington, with Althea Bennett's cookies tucked under a Secret Service agent's arm, Ford gave two more speeches and lingered long with his audiences as if he was trying to fortify himself for the disappointing ordeal he knew lay ahead.

He ended the campaign stronger than ever, the way he used to when he played football. There was one incredible day on the West Coast when he put in eighteen hours, starting with a visit with Richard Nixon in the Long Beach Hospital. There were rallies, conferences, television appearances. In Fresno he tried to buck up the faltering candidacy of Bob Mathias, who had won the decathlon in the 1948 London Olympics. Ford fox-trotted at the Portland Urban League dance. He sold his cuff links for charity, hiked a football through the presidential legs for another bidder, went to a basketball game and ended the evening at a party for his official photographer, David Hume Kennerly, whom Ford pronounced "Washington's number one bachelor." But he had little more that he could say, and there were no more Grand Rapids nostalgia baths. The people out beyond the hometown were hard-eyed, scared and bruised from the long Watergate ordeal, the faltering economy and unanswered questions about their new President. "We want strong, stalwart people in Congress who will bite the bullet and not fade away when they ought to be strong," Ford said. Very few appeared moved by the appeal.

On election night Ford sat before the screens of four television sets and watched the avalanche that Tip O'Neill had warned about roll over him and over the Republican party. The Democrats gained four governors, three senators and forty-three House seats. Here and there Ford was credited with an assist. Senator Robert Dole of Kansas said Ford had helped him cut Democrats down in Wichita by appearing at a rally there the Saturday before the election. Utah's Senator-elect Jake Garn announced that Ford had provided him his winning margin. In Oklahoma, Henry Bellmon pulled it out by an eyelash. But the pileup of losses was immense. Paul Goebel went under in Grand Rapids and so did athlete Mathias in California. Iowa's Wiley Mayne and Virginia's Stanford Parris lost; both were men whom Ford had

pointedly gone to help. There were many others. "The people have spoken," said a chastened Ford, "and for twenty-six years I have accepted the verdict of the people, which is the essence of our system of free government." It was a distressing time for the new President, so finely tuned to American politics.

But worrying about what might have been or should have been is not a pastime for successful politicians. Defeats are studied, then put on the shelf. In the White House it is even more important that the men look ahead instead of behind. The prospect for new adventure, for new diversion is endless, and in two weeks Ford was headed for Asia, his first extended trip abroad as President. He planned ceremonial visits to Japan and Korea, then a stop at Vladivostok in the Soviet Union to meet Communist Party Chief Leonid Brezhnev and talk about further limits on nuclear arms.

It was not all that different from his domestic campaigning. In fact, it was international politicking of a sort, lending the powerful presence of the United States President to bolster his hosts, politicians in their own right with the full range of survival problems with which any man in the business must contend. In Japan Ford was to fulfill an obligation contracted by Richard Nixon to buck up Prime Minister Kakuei Tanaka. Tanaka's government had been shaken needlessly by Nixon's obsession for secrecy when the United States made its opening with Red China without any advance warning for Japan, then had unexpectedly devalued the American dollar. Ford now had the job of saying he was sorry and rebuilding good relations. Tanaka was, in fact, on his way out as prime minister, but Ford designed his visit as a personal gesture to honor the Japanese people.

Before Ford arrived there had been protests and the American embassy had been bombed. The anger was directed mostly at Tanaka, who was blamed for the faltering Japanese

economy and was also under fire for the personal fortune he had amassed during his years of public service. The presidential visit was being used to attract attention to the dissatisfaction. Security for Ford's stay was heavy. But despite the restrictions on his movements, Ford, through television and the Japanese newspapers, could be scrutinized by the people. He was ideal for this role—tall, polite, rugged and smiling. He could stride impressively across the red carpets laid down for him, looking as if he liked the routine. It was much like hometown politics. His presence counted. There was very little business to do, most of the difficulties over trade, energy and nuclear arms already being worked on by lesser diplomats. Ford was to be on display.

On November 18 Ford's jet shuddered through the turbulent winds off Mount Fuji and settled on the Tokyo runway. He choppered over the city and spent his first night in the Akasaka Palace, sleeping in a huge pink-canopied bed. Ford's crusted pipes and pouch of Cavendish tobacco were soon scattered about the royal premises, the mixings of a good American martini faithfully furnished each evening so he could relax after the speeches and banquets and tedious formalities of the long days.

Much to Ford's delight, the Japanese had done their homework and throughout his visit the ceremonial bands played the Michigan fight song. An American with the instincts of Ford could not be held behind the police barricades for all of the three days. Before the first day was over, Ford broke ranks and sought out a group of Japanese, who eagerly shook his hand, sometimes as many as three or four of them clutching him at once. Towering over his hosts, Ford dutifully posed for pic-

In a flawless ballet of position and protocol, a White House aide, right, rushes up to put the presidential seal on the front of the podium just as the President steps up to deliver his speech. This scene is in the Muehlebach Hotel, Kansas City, Missouri. Local Republicans had preceded Ford at the speakers' stand during the breakfast fund-raiser.

In Sioux Falls, South Dakota, Ford stands up in the presidential limousine to wave to people along the street as he heads for the arena to deliver a campaign speech. The bombproof, bulletproof automobile made by the Ford Motor Company is one of the special playthings of Chief Executives. The roof opens to allow the President to be seen and to see the folks. The contingent of Secret Service agents trotted alongside in this case because the distance was short. When weather is bad or there are security questions, the President can stay comfortably inside but deliver his greetings to the crowds through a special loudspeaker built into the car.

Where are we? Sometimes the presidential caravan travels so far and so fast that the sense of place and direction is almost lost. This is never so true as on a political junket. On this day the Ford blitz for Republican congressional candidates had begun in Missouri, moved through South Dakota and Nebraska and wound up in the evening at the Indianapolis Convention Center in Indiana. In the VIP suite, Ford paused for a few minutes to phone the White House and answer those urgent questions that had piled up for him in his absence. Here, he talks for a minute with Press Secretary Ron Nessen. The silhouette is classic Ford, easily identifiable to those in the presidential party. His trousers are slightly flared, his coat tailored with Italian vents. Before he went on down to talk to the huge crowd below, Ford satisfied himself that the nation was tranquil and he could go back to his role as Republican party leader.

Those people who encounter a President on the move rarely forget it. None are more impressed than the kids lucky enough to be pressed into ceremonial service. The boy scout honor guard at Greenville, South Carolina, head toward destiny in this picture, a bit out of step but plainly aware of their responsibility. They are given a stern look by the Marine member of the President's contingent, standing under the tip of one of the rotors of the helicopter that will take Ford to his rally site. Air Force One has had the sky to itself as it descended to the runway, a security precaution for traveling Presidents. Even to hardened travel hands, the approach of the beautiful silver and blue plane is a majestic sight.

The guardian of the President's health, Dr. William Lukash, surveys his charge from the tarmac at Lincoln, Nebraska. Ford has just landed in Air Force One and is in the middle of the cluster of people in the distance. He is shaking the hands of those who had come to witness his arrival. Lukash is never far away from the President, no matter where Ford travels. The doctor has assistants who stand in for him when he takes time off. The black bag at Lukash's feet is a special physician's kit, stuffed with the usual pills and potions but also containing emergency gear should Ford (or important members of the party) need medication or quick treatment.

tures, held his talks with the government officials, made the necessary small talk ("We have a large group of press people. More wanted to come. It's important that the press report this historic visit").

Time and time again he raised a full glass in a toast and said the correct things ("Some of our finest citizens have a Japanese ancestry"). He admired the beautiful silk kimonos of the Japanese women who came to the official dinners. And he savored the magnificent wines (Château Lafite Rothschild 1964), one of many signs of Japan's affluence and sophistication. He was politely curious about almost everything, once asking Tanaka how the sumo wrestlers got so big, and even managing to look interested in the reply. "It's the kind of food they eat," answered Tanaka.

Ford was treated to an afternoon of gymnastics, taking a particular interest in the small judo contestants; one twelve-year-old American boy won presidential plaudits despite the fact that he got thrown by his Japanese opponent. In Japan, Ford's visit was a success. In America, where more somber economic news was reported every day, there were growing questions about the wisdom of his being away. But Ford's private worries about what was happening back in the United States were never allowed to intrude on his public performance in Japan. "The American people have faced some difficult times in their history," Ford said at the Japan Press Club. "They know that they will face others. Their burdens are enormous, at home and abroad. Some observers—including American observers—say that the Americans have lost their confidence, their sense of responsibility, and their creativity. It is not true."

Ford flew on to Kyoto, site of the ancient Japanese palaces. He was pure tourist. At the Imperial Palace's Pond Garden he stood on a stone bridge and clapped his hands in an effort to attract the trained golden carp. When the fish failed to respond the first time, Ford laughed and tried again. Still no carp. At the other end of the pond Ford mounted another bridge and clapped some more. This time he was successful. A lone fish swam within presidential orbit and Ford was immensely pleased. The episode was carefully preserved and catalogued by the reporters present.

He padded in slippers through the graceful Nijo Castle, moved out into the garden and stopped to listen to seven girls playing the koto, a sixteenth-century stringed instrument. When they finished Ford asked if he could try to pluck a note or two. He could not get the metal pick on his big finger, but finally grasped it between his thumb and forefinger and struck a few twangs, which delighted his tour guides and the girls, who giggled appreciatively. "You are a very good player," said one of the girls to the President, who gave her one of his best smiles. Such are the duties of the most powerful man in the world when he is on tour—sometimes inane, often boring, but always required. When Ford left, he was his kindly Grand Rapids self. "The culture of Japan certainly is an inspiration," he said. "This has been a wonderful trip—couldn't have been better." Perhaps it was not the most eloquent testimonial, but it was Jerry Ford and he meant it, which makes up for a lot.

His stop in Korea was about the minimum that protocol would allow. President Park Chung Hee's repressive regime was undergoing criticism in America and, besides, Ford was hurrying on to the Soviet Union for his session with Leonid Brezhnev. Ford stopped to see the American troops still guarding the thirty-seventh parallel between North and South Korea and there he got a little advice from a GI. While he was eating a lunch of hamburgers, cottage cheese and potato chips, the soldier shouted out, "Tell those Russians who's number one." Ford smiled and shook the man's hand.

Telling people who was number one was not Ford's way. But the GI's remark underscored the seriousness of the coming encounter with the Soviet leader. While Secretary of State Kissinger had worked out the sense of the new arms limitation agreement in October, no figures had been set, and the real meaning of the Ford-Brezhnev get-together was in mutual personal assessment.

I called Kissinger late one night in Kyoto for a last-minute reading on what lay ahead. It would take some time before we would really learn the true meaning of Vladivostok, Kissinger said. "The important thing is the impression of the President that Brezhnev takes back to the Kremlin. If he goes back feeling that Ford is a man he can trust, someone with whom he can have a special relationship and yet not push around, then it will be a success." Kissinger sounded tired. And Ford looked bushed. Besides the doubt about having the Asian junket just when so much bad news was breaking back in the United States, the question of conducting any kind of serious talks with the Soviet Union in such a state of fatigue was raised in the traveling press corps.

Brezhnev flew to Siberia early. His plane had been grounded by a blizzard and he had journeyed on into Vladivostok by train. But he had a good night's sleep and a full morning to ponder his strategy before greeting Ford at the fighter base near Ussuriysk, a city in the Primorye region, which is just beyond the border of Siberia.

Ford had read all the detailed briefing books that Kissinger had furnished him, thick volumes of facts and figures on nuclear weapons, the prime area of discussion for the session. In addition, he had spent hours back in Washington and on Air Force One discussing the personality of Brezhnev and the gamesmanship required. While it was obvious to the American party that Ford would not be as experienced, as facile or as (continued on page 112)

An early political disillusionment. These young enthusiasts had come to the rally in Greensville, South Carolina, with banners and hopes high. They had a long hour to wait until the President arrived.

The President and his people, the basic ingredients of politics. At Rock Hill, South Carolina, on a windy, sunny day in mid-October, Ford comes on the stand at the Rock Hill Mall with a smile and a wave to give candidate Len Phillips the presidential blessing. Ford was always a casual candidate, coat unbuttoned and trousers wrinkled from flying. In this he contrasted with Nixon, who never seemed creased or unbuttoned no matter how strenuous the schedule. Far right, above: The people who have come to the Rock Hill rally listen intently as the President makes his pitch for the Grand Old Party and Phillips. In Phillips' case, the Presidential enthusiasm did not work. He lost. Far right, below: A youthful crowd in the Sioux Falls Arena reach to touch Ford's hand after his speech. Such direct contact remains a rare privilege even in these jet days. While most Americans grow intimately familiar with the electronic presidential image, only a tiny fraction of this nation's 210 million people ever actually see a President in the flesh.

Even though the 1974 electoral defeat was predicted, Gerald Ford and his wife and aides were not fully prepared for the impact of the landslide that hit them. Perhaps no politician ever is. There lurks in the back of his mind the idea that the polls and the pundits are wrong, that some miracle will occur and bring his party out on top. For Ford on the night of November 5, the predictions were all too true, the expected defeat starkly evident even at the beginning of the evening. Right: The Fords sit in their private quarters watching television as the first bad news comes. Ford made no effort to feign good humor, and was a somber man throughout the ordeal. Left: Back in the Oval Office after a conference with his senior staff members, he watches the results as reported on the four Washington TV stations. While some staff members expressed bitterness at the Democratic victory, even at how it was reported by the network anchormen, Ford did not. He accepted the results for what they were and approved a statement given by Press Secretary Nessen acknowledging the debacle.

Overleaf: Ford in his suite in Tokyo's Akasaka Palace on the first stop of his overseas tour.

WELCOME

The first of President Gerald Ford's overseas adventures began in Japan. And his first important ceremony was the meeting with Emperor Hirohito in front of the Akasaka Palace in Tokyo. Right: The two men listen to the national anthems before trooping the line of the honor guard and meeting the diplomats who had been assembled. It was in this ceremony that Ford's too-short pants were noticed. Also, his wing-tip collar was of a different style than that worn by the Emperor, which caused ripples in the State Department's protocol section. Ford hardly noticed. He marched through the formal routines with unflagging graciousness and energy. Left: In Korea, the airport portraits of the two Presidents that hung from the control tower form a backdrop to one of the armed guards who were always nearby during Ford's short stay. President Park Chung Hee greeted Ford, then gave him a traditional motorcade into the heart of Seoul. Hundreds of thousands of Koreans lined the route and there was not a single unfavorable incident in that heavily policed city.

In Kyoto, Japan, right, Ford pauses during sightseeing to shake hands with some Japanese people. He had just toured the Gold Pavilion, a reconstruction of a historic fourteenth-century Buddhist temple that was destroyed by fire in 1950. Because of concern for security, Ford had few chances during his Japanese visit to see or be seen by the people and whenever he found a group like this he insisted on going through his political ritual. At least one woman is extremely happy. Far right: Ford takes lunch with the American troops in Camp Casey, near the border between North and South Korea. It was an American menu of hamburgers, cottage cheese and potato chips, and Ford ate it all.

imaginative as Nixon, his own special strengths would be important. Ford had a better knowledge of the arms field than most people credited him with. His coolness and low temper were assets. He also, as his aides had noted in his previous meetings, always searched for a genuine human connection with the men with whom he talked. Nixon was never able to look a man in the eye very long. The former President programed himself rigidly before he went to his summit talks and when the discussion veered unexpectedly he sometimes got upset and nervous. Ford was more adaptable. His openness, his bearish frame and his love of the outdoors and athletics also seemed ready-made for the Russians.

Even before Ford's plane touched down, the American correspondents standing in the thin cold of Vozdvizhenka airport had a preview of the contact between the two principals. Brezhnev drove up with Andrei Gromyko, the foreign minister, Anatoly Dobrynin, the ambassador to the United States, and a few other aides. Smoking a cigarette, he strolled down the ramp in a heavy black coat, a gray wool astrakhan on his head. He looked in good health and ready for a tussle. When he saw the press, he walked over and shouted, "To the Russians I say, 'Hello.' To the Americans I say, 'Okay.'" Peter Lisagor called out, "Has the Chairman ever played football?" The newsmen chortled and Brezhnev grinned when the translation was made. "Right half," came back the answer and Brezhnev took a few running steps in place, declaring he was "warming up." He walked on down the tarmac, then came back. Pointing to the camouflaged bunkers that dotted the airfield, the kind used for ammunition storage in the United States, Brezhnev said, "You probably think those contain bombs. You are wrong. They have vegetables. Toma-

toes." There was more guffawing. It was plain that Brezhnev was set to take the measure of Ford, whose plane was just taxiing to a halt.

The President rushed down the ramp with a big smile, his hand extended to the Soviet Chairman. There were shoulder slaps and greetings, then somebody produced the mink hats that had been given to Ford and Kissinger by Dobrynin back in Washington. The group shuffled toward the press again, trying to make small talk. "I understand that you are quite an expert on soccer," Ford said. "Yes, I play the left side, but I haven't played in a long time," Brezhnev replied. "I haven't played football for a long time, either," said Ford. "I wasn't very fast, but I could hold the line." Ford, it was evident, was never going to be able to match repartee with Brezhnev, who is a natural mimic and wit. But the important thing was that Ford held the American dignity and sense of firm purpose.

On the train heading for Vladivostok, Ford settled in with the Russians and looked out over the expanse of gently rolling country covered with snow. It was a beautiful scene. Ford chatted about the problems of snow falling in Washington, D.C. "And that will be our first deal," snorted Brezhnev, waving his cigarette. "We will send you Soviet snowplows." Gromyko interjected, "At a good low price." Then it was time for work. Immediately after the reporters had left the special car, the doors were closed and the talk turned to the serious matter of nuclear weapons and how to control them, eventually reduce them. For almost sixteen out of the next thirty hours, Ford would be engaged in this somber discussion. "We have to compress three days' talks into one," said Kissinger.

The train made its leisurely way down to the Okeanskaya sanitarium, the meeting site, which overlooked the water. The area had been closed to Westerners for twenty-six years. Old and new Russia were intermingled in the snowscape. Factories, barracks, huge apartment complexes crowded the countryside in places.

But for the most part, there were groves of birch and meandering streams partially covered with ice. Here and there boys skied through the trees, younger children played with wooden sleds. Some of the homes were old peasant cottages with weathered wood siding and bright colored shutters and picket fences, remnants from another time in this vast land.

For Ford the next day and a half was a blur of bargaining, brief interludes for rest, meals delayed and then skipped as the talk went on. He got a swim in an indoor pool near his dacha, which probably did more to restore his energy than anything else. He and Brezhnev clowned with a wolfskin coat that Ford had been given in Anchorage, Alaska, on the way over. Brezhnev wrestled the coat on and said he wanted it; Ford gave it to him.

Sometime Saturday night Brezhnev wrote out on a piece of paper the limits that the Soviet Union would accept on missiles and nuclear warheads and this was the basis for the agreement that was announced the next day. Ford and Henry Kissinger went for one of their walks in the snow to be sure of their position. A half moon lighted the landscape and lent an eerie beauty to the scene. Everything seemed to be going well.

That night, when the President finally got to sit down and eat with his staff, he was in a good mood. He tackled a steaming bowl of Russian salyanka soup, chewed on some cold cuts and asked for vanilla ice cream. Then he called it a day. It was 1:30 a.m. "Brezhnev would be surprised if he knew I plan to get up at four in the morning to listen to a football game," Ford had joked before retiring. But even Ford proved not quite up to that, despite his keen interest in the Michigan–Ohio State game.

There was more bargaining through the next day and then sometime in the afternoon it was done. The two superpowers had agreed to put a cap on the arms race, limiting missile

Perhaps no American has been engaged in so many complicated diplomatic meetings as Secretary of State Henry Kissinger, shown with President Ford as the two walked toward the opening conference with Japan's Prime Minister Kakuei Tanaka in the Akasaka Palace. The fund of experience and knowledge that Kissinger carries in his head is invaluable and Ford, while not exactly a novice at these things, needed all the help he could get—he was in a new league. He listened to Kissinger's advice, which included not only suggestions on the substance of the talks but personal assessments of the men Ford would face and what tactics might be employed in the debates. Ford had done a great deal of homework for this meeting. He had gone through the heavy black briefing books that the State Department traditionally prepares. He had read countless memos which had followed and spent hours in Washington and on Air Force One being briefed by Kissinger and the other experts. In such encounters knowledge is power and a President can never have enough.

In Vladivostok, right, above, Leonid Brezhnev does a bit of clowning with President Ford's wolfskin coat, which had been given to Ford in Anchorage, Alaska, on his way to Asia. Ford had put the coat on after arriving at his seaside dacha in Vladivostok, worn it to walk the few yards to the summit site. Brezhnev had admired the coat when Ford came in the door so the President took it off and presented it to the Communist Party chief. Brezhnev did not seem quite sure what was happening and he gave the coat back to Ford, who once again presented it to Brezhnev when he left Vladivostok the following day. Right, below: Ford goes through his hat routine shortly after coming down the ramp upon arrival at Vozdvizhenka airport, Ussuriysk, on the edge of Siberia. Anatoly Dobrynin, the Soviet's U.S. ambassador, had given mink hats to both Ford and Kissinger back in Washington. Ford raced down the ramp bareheaded but soon put on his new hat as Brezhnev commented. Far right: Ford gives the universal political signal of thanks and joy at the end of the Vladivostok summit. Tired but jubilant, having just signed the agreement putting a cap on the missile race, Ford paused on the ramp before ducking into Air Force One and heading home via Alaska.

launchers to 2,400 and those with multiple warheads to 1,320 though the figures would not be announced for several days so Ford could brief Congress.

It was a major step toward disarmament, that ideal of modern civilization that has shimmered so deceptively on the far horizon since the end of World War II.

Riding back to the sanitarium after releasing a communiqué, Press Secretary Nessen was overheard talking to Henry Kissinger about the press's reaction. "I think they were dazzled," Nessen said. "I think they were amazed. I don't think they were expecting an agreement like this. The President will be returning home in triumph."

It was overkill, the kind that had gotten Nixon into so much trouble. There were unanswered questions about the agreement, untold stories about how Ford and Brezhnev really got along. Some reporters were reminded that after the 1961 summit in Vienna, Nikita Khrushchev went back to Moscow convinced that Kennedy could be intimidated, and thereupon Khrushchev devised his plan for putting missiles into Cuba. The long-range results of Vladivostok were still to be determined.

Kissinger understood the hazards of too much optimism, although he was the one who came up with the slogans "breakthrough" and "cap on the arms race." In the car he told Nessen, "I think the President should be modest. The agreement speaks for itself. The back of this [the arms race] is broken."

A sense of Brezhnev's personal measure of Ford was missing. Brezhnev had been jovial, flattering and respectful. But Ford never did trust himself to be alone with the Soviet leader as Nixon had done. Kissinger was at Ford's elbow every step of the way. Often Kissinger did the talking while Ford listened. At first the Russians were puzzled. Can Brezhnev push Ford around? an American asked a member of the Soviet delegation. "There's nothing to push around," the Russian said. "He sits there and says very little." But by the time the summit ended, the notion (or the Kremlin signals) had changed. "Your President is a steady man," said one Russian. "Straight, direct, normal and pleasant. He needs training in foreign affairs. With a little seasoning he can play in the major leagues."

They signed the agreements on Sunday afternoon in the modest solarium where the meetings had been held. The champagne was hustled in by waiters; the participants formed a semicircle and toasted their accomplishment. Brezhnev gave Ford a quick tour of downtown Vladivostok, and once again the presidential party was on the train headed back to the airport, this time minus the Russians, who were staying behind to rest and discuss their assessment of the new President.

Nessen could not contain his joy at Ford's achievement. "It was something that Nixon couldn't do in three years, but Ford did it in three months," he said. "I don't know what it was—they [Brezhnev and Ford] hit it off." In the world of international diplomacy such talk is unwise at almost any time. Booby traps lie around every corner, and today's triumph often turns into tomorrow's disaster. The old hands know that events must speak for themselves. Nessen had not yet learned that fact.

When Ford was asked on the train what he thought, he felt a touch of the euphoria too. "Just good negotiating," he said. "Good give and take." The trainload of tired, happy Americans rolled on through the snowy fields of Far Eastern Russia. Ford, grinning, posed for pictures with the train hostesses and other Russian functionaries who had served him along the summit way. Then he was aboard Air Force One and headed back home to a land that was in many ways a lot colder than the edge of Siberia.

"Private" Life in the White House

Family appeal. Betty Ford does her best
to make the point to her husband that she
does not approve of son Steve's going
to rodeo school. Since he already was in
the Wyoming school, there was little
either of them could do. Ford brought
the matter before his wife in Aspen
Lodge at Camp David after a swim, and
just before he was going off to play
tennis in his red Marine Corps sweat
suit. As he perused a secret report on
Henry Kissinger's latest meeting with
Soviet Chief Brezhnev, Ford remarked
casually that he had heard from Steve
and Steve was going to the rodeo
school. Mrs. Ford stood up, puzzled.
"He didn't ask me," she said. "He
didn't ask me either," answered the
President. Betty Ford pushed the
Kissinger report aside, sat on her husband's lap, mussed his hair and suggested that it was something they
should not let their son do. "I don't
want him all broken up in rodeos," she
said. "I've given him some good advice," the President said. "Get gentle
cows and old horses." Then he added,
"He's grown up and you know how
well he has taken our advice on
everything else."

When Gerald Ford became President, his salary more than tripled (from $62,500 to $200,000) and his living quarters went from nine rooms to forty. His staff jumped from thirty to nearly five hundred, while his commutation time dropped from thirty to three and a half minutes—roughly the time it takes a tall man with an open stride to go down in the residence elevator, along the ground-floor hall, through the arcade and to his desk. There were no trucks or buses or traffic snarls along the way. Instead, only an encounter with Dr. William Lukash, the President's genial physician, who gave him a quick once-over each morning for color and mood. In almost any season except the depths of winter, Ford would see fresh blooms (tulips, chrysanthemums, hyacinths, crocuses) growing in the Rose Garden beside the arcade.

Ford's family was closer too. True, his three sons were all away from home, but the marvels of the White House telephone were soon discovered and there was perhaps more talk among them than ever before. His daughter Susan, seventeen, had been a boarding student at Holton-Arms School in nearby Bethesda, Maryland, when Ford was in the House and, later, Vice-President. But when the Nixons vacated the White House and the Fords moved in, Susan moved "home" to a bright third-story bedroom suite. She carefully supervised the transfer from her family's Alexandria home of all of her two dozen potted plants, taking with good grace her mother's admonition that at the White House she would have to take care of them ("Don't I always?") and then wondering what would happen to the plants when her expanding social schedule kept her away from the White House. "Well, I'll find somebody. Maybe Mr. Harriston [a White House doorman]; he's so nice." Susan had some animal problems too—her Siamese cat, Shan. But Mrs. Ford assured her daughter that Shan would be welcome anyplace in the private preserve.

Just to be sure that the world was warned that while some things were changing, others decidedly would not, Susan declared, "I'll never throw away my blue jeans." The Ford kids were brought up with the idea that each is an individual, and that delicate balance was not to be altered by the White House residence. "Wouldn't it be great to have a party with the Beach Boys or Bette Midler in the White House?" mused Susan in the first days. A few months later, her brother Jack almost made that desire come true. He invited George Harrison, the former Beatle, Harrison's father and assorted members of the musical troupe to the White House for lunch. Young Ford, a forestry student at Utah State University, had met Harrison in Utah, where he was performing, had enjoyed a backstage chat in which the singer had cleared up Ford's identity for a third party present with this explanation: "His father runs the country."

They lunched in the third-floor solarium on a menu heavy with vegetables and salad to accommodate Harrison's vegetarianism, then went to the Oval Office to meet "Father." The President and the ex-Beatle exchanged buttons. Harrison got a WIN button, which he wore at his concert that night. Ford received a button with the word OM, Sanskrit for "wholeness." And Susan got the job of showing the group through the White House because, as it turned out, Jack had never spent a night there in the four months his father had been President. "Out there [Utah] is much more home than here," he said. "A lot of people have grandiose ideas about what the White House is, but it's basically a box with a lot of rooms in it. It's nice but I wouldn't build a home like this."

Neither would Betty Ford. But since it came her way she started from the beginning to make the best of it. "I want the children to have their friends here and have fun," she said. "It's time now that we get back to simplicity." Susan's blue jeans became a Ford trademark, and son Steve washed his yellow jeep out back on the drive, which is more accustomed to long black limousines.

When one White House aide helping Mrs. Ford plan the residence suggested it could become very lonely in the private quarters, Mrs. Ford set the record straight. "Not for me... If I don't have anything scheduled I'll call up friends and have them come for lunch. After all, that's what it is for." And it was not necessarily her husband she wanted to join her over there for lunch. "I can't imagine that—he's too busy," she said. "I don't want him for lunch." Such candor brought chortles from appreciative wives all across the nation. Betty Ford was frank about just everything. "We have shared the same bed for twenty-five years and we're not about to change that," she also remarked. But she was immensely pleased at having additional space for dressing rooms. "Now Jerry can get dressed in a room of his own. For years I've tried to sleep while he was getting dressed—now he won't have to tiptoe. He's always been an early riser. That is the part of the day he really enjoys—he gets his breakfast and reads....I wouldn't dare intrude. ...I can't imagine anything worse than starting off the day with conversation."

The Fords, as with others who had lived there, found that the White House and the life of the presidency focused their energies more than anything they had ever undertaken. Their interests and their personal activities were helped along by an amazing staff, which could furnish just about every vital service (serve cocktails for thirty unexpected guests, build a snowman on the South Lawn) or improvise it with a smile.

The important impact of the White House on family life was the closeness. Living on the White House grounds is somewhat like living in a small Southern village. Everything is within walking distance. The family members can see each other frequently in the course of the day's work and give each other a wave or a friendly yell.

Some days when Susan got home from school she took a romp with Liberty, the golden retriever that she and David Kennerly, the White House photographer, bought for her father. And while out on the lawn, if the spirit so moved her, she would pop into the Oval Office to see her dad. Almost always if he was set to travel in the late afternoon, Susan would see to it to be on hand and walk with him from his office to the waiting helicopter about twenty-five yards up the drive. Susan recruited kitchen aide Frank Blair to help her scrub down Liberty, and there was always someone around to give her pointers on training the dog.

One of the first things Susan discovered was the White House movie theater and the right to order up any new film. The place became a favorite haunt of the teenager and her friends. They settled in to see *The Sting* and *That's Entertainment,* and a few others a little more adult.

Mrs. Ford kept an eye out of her dressing room or the big arched window of the West Sitting Room, where the family really lived. When she saw the President down in the Rose Garden she would thump on the glass and give him a big wave or two. When Halloween came around there was a fifty-pound jack-o-lantern grinning out the sitting room window to cheer the President or anybody else who happened to be down below. The jack-o-lantern was the handiwork of secretary Nancy Howe and Robert Blundy, who worked in the flower shop on the ground floor.

When Mrs. Ford heard the helicopter coming down on the South Lawn

from Andrews Air Force Base, she almost always ran for the Truman Balcony and gave the President a welcome-home flutter. He always returned the greeting. On the nights when he walked home from work, he gave his wife a kiss, asked, "And how was your day?" Then he listened for a few minutes. They usually had a drink together, then went on to dinner in the private dining room. After that, if there was no formal entertaining or other activity, they settled into the President's study. Ford's old blue leather easy chair had been put there, his political pictures and mementoes hung on the wall along with photos of the kids. It was just Jerry Ford's room where he could watch television or read a bit. When he was in there with Mrs. Ford the two of them usually sipped tea and went about their homework—signing pictures, coordinating schedules, reading memos or talking about the children. There were certain times when the couple insisted on their special rights. They wedged in a very private lunch on their twenty-sixth wedding anniversary, and White House pastry chef Heinz Bender sculpted some exquisite hearts out of ice cream to give the table a special flair. At Christmas, despite the heavy load of diplomatic, congressional and press parties they had scheduled, the Fords set aside evenings for family dinners, and on those nights they shut out the rest of the world. They also insisted on their traditional period of family skiing at Vail, and though they were forced by security considerations to take a larger, less centrally located home, their routine was much the same as in other years.

Back in Alexandria, the Fords had been used to entertaining with barbecues out around the pool or at buffet suppers where guests could move through the small rooms of their modest home. In the White House the fare quickly expanded and improved in quality. Both the President and his wife found the food service to be a delight. The

The President's easy chair in his study, brought from his Alexandria, Virginia, home. It is adorned with his favorite self-characterization up to that point in mid-October.

White House kitchens were ready with anything, from Mrs. Ford's soft-boiled breakfast eggs to the President's salads, of which he took two helpings most times when the family ate by themselves. His special preference was to have finely sliced onions mixed into the salads. Ford described himself as a "meat and potatoes" man and that was essentially correct. His wife went him one better, suggesting he had a cast iron stomach that could withstand any assault—and had. The White House "meat and potatoes" came out a little fancier than standard fare, but it was based on plain American ideas. There was breast of capon with rice; calves' liver with onions; sirloin; filet of sole; grilled lamb chops; and filet mignon. Chef Henry Haller had never heard of the President's favorite dessert—pecan ice cream with peach slices on top. In fact, confided Haller, he had never even imagined such a combination. But he put it together to please the Chief and tried it himself. He reported it was pretty tasty.

There was a good-natured tug of war between the White House kitchen and the President's physician regarding a matter of some extra weight. Dr. Lukash put an 1,800-calorie limit on Ford's daily intake, designing the schedule so that the President could get one or two martinis over lots of ice and indulge himself on Sunday mornings with an old favorite—waffles with sour cream, strawberries and maple syrup.

To counteract the waffles and sour cream (and make up for the lack of a swimming pool), Ford had an exercise bicycle set up in his study. In the mornings the President spent a few minutes pumping, then worked some tension devices to strengthen his knees, both of which had been operated on for football injuries. Lukash's aim was to get the President down to 195 pounds, and he achieved it by November. There was

a minimum of complaining from such a physical-fitness buff as Ford. Once or twice he muttered, "Boy, am I ever hungry." But he had little time on his schedule for such extraneous thoughts. He also allowed as how "riding that exercise bicycle is the most boring thing in the world," and all kinds of plans were devised for getting a glassed-in swimming pool installed on the South Lawn. The first attempts to get voluntary donors for the pool were thwarted by Ford's own policy declarations in which he called on Americans to exercise more austerity. He decided that he could forgo a new swimming pool.

But Ford soon discovered some of the other pleasures at the command of a President. He got out on the White House tennis court, exhorting his partners to give it the old college try. He sampled the pool table in the basement. At Camp David, the presidential mountaintop retreat sixty miles northwest of Washington, he strolled in the woods or romped with Liberty over the cleared acres. There he had a magnificent heated swimming pool, which he used whenever he was in residence. Totally adventurous, he could not resist taking a turn on the trampoline when he saw his daughter try it. There were horses to ride, a skeet range, three holes of golf, more tennis courts, snowmobiles, an archery range, and it was certain that if Gerald Ford ever mentioned he wanted to try horseshoes or tiddlywinks, the Navy, which runs Camp David, would produce the necessary installation in nothing flat.

So lathered with services and perquisites and money has the White House become that some people have honestly wondered if we do not give our Presidents too much. Certainly it is time to dispel some of the old mythology about what a man-killing job being president has to be. To be sure, it has its moments of frustration, and the burden at times must grow almost intolerable for a sensitive man. Yet for men in the power business, being President is a

Mr. and Mrs. Ford dance after the state dinner for Austria's Chancellor Bruno Kreisky.

natural ambition and not that awesome a challenge. No recent President has been dragged kicking and screaming into the Oval Office. The people who wanted the job have lined up outside the gate. There were some figures compiled a few years ago by historian Thomas Bailey showing that Presidents generally outlived their Vice-Presidents, the men they ran against to get into office and, finally, their wives. The figures will have to be revised because there are now five former first ladies alive, and only one ex-President. But the principle holds—being President is not a bad job.

"I feel great," Ford said one night aboard Air Force One, talking to Saul Pett of the Associated Press. He confessed that a year or two earlier, when he was still on the Hill, he was feeling "a little bored." But now, Ford remarked to Pett, "the old adrenaline is going."

The new energy flooded into all parts of Washington. The Kennedys had more elegance and the Johnsons more flavor, but the Fords used their openness and natural grace with telling effect.

Leon Jaworski, the special prosecutor who had so painfully secured the evidence that toppled Richard Nixon, was asked to the White House, where he had not been welcome since the days of his old friend LBJ. Jaworski had been at the White House during the previous year as he pressed the case against Nixon. But those visits had been short, serious sessions, and he had never got back upstairs in the residence. When Polish Communist leader Edward Gierek came to town and the Fords put on a dinner, Jaworski, the son of a Polish immigrant, got an invitation to come as a regular guest. Up in the state rooms, where there was music and champagne, Jaworski commented that it

felt good again. There was life back in the old building.

The state dinner for Austrian Chancellor Bruno Kreisky was a reunion of many people who had been deliberately excluded by other Presidents. Lee Bouvier Radziwill, the sister of Jacqueline Kennedy Onassis, came as the date of architect Philip Johnson. The irrepressible Barbara Howar, who had been cut off eight years earlier in the Johnson administration, returned with a smile and several quips as the date of United Press International correspondent Richard Growald. And there, too, was William O. Douglas, the very man whom Ford had tried to impeach. Justice Douglas looked around the place and declared that he had no hard feelings against the President, who had given him a warm greeting. "This used to be my old stomping grounds," said the seventy-six-year-old New Dealer. "When FDR was President I was here all the time. I'm glad to be home tonight."

The Fords ventured beyond the White House in the evenings, something that the Nixons and the Johnsons rarely did in Washington. At the Kennedy Center they helped celebrate the tenth anniversary of the founding of the National Endowment for the Arts, the President confessing to his audience his newness to an appreciation of the arts: "I am a converted individual [to the arts]—and I don't apologize for it. Converts are oftentimes known as more ardent advocates than those brought up in a religion." And then he remembered the giant Calder sculpture that is the pride of Grand Rapids, standing massively in the heart of the city. "I'm proud of it, but I haven't found out with any specificity what he [Calder] was trying to tell us. I point it out to all visitors—including the Secret Service —and tell them it's nothing they should be worried about."

From the presidential box that night he watched what he called "my kind of show." It was *Mack and Mabel,*

the story of Mack Sennett and Mabel Normand in early Hollywood. When it was over, the President and Mrs. Ford went backstage, joking with the cast. "A man who is married to a modern dancer can't be all bad," quipped one actor. "I liked the tap-dancing," said Ford to producer David Merrick. When composer Jerry Herman volunteered his services as a campaign songwriter, Ford rejoined, "I'll see you in two years." The President wished them all good luck on the new show and actor Tom Batten came right back: "Good luck on *your* new show." As the Fords walked out, the cast broke into applause. Robert Preston, the show's star, watched them go and summed it up by saying what most people just think at such times: "That was exciting, goddamn it."

When the boys from the Hill wanted Ford to come out to the third annual Congressional Golf Tournament at Andrews Air Force Base, he was ready. He played in a foursome with Majority Leader O'Neill, House Minority Leader John Rhodes (who replaced Ford in the job) and GOP whip Leslie Arends. Ford, an 18 handicapper, sliced the first one off the fairway and through some observers. He got applauded anyway by the people who dodged his ball. Ford knew better. He tried another and put it about 180 yards straight down the middle.

When O'Neill lighted up a big cigar, Ford warned the rotund Irishman from Boston not "to asphyxiate me." O'Neill didn't. But Ford, like any weekend golfer who doesn't get quite enough practice, had his problems. He ended up once in a grove of trees, dropped the ball nicely from ninety yards to within twelve feet of the pin, then missed the putt by an inch. Ford was given a 49 for his ten holes, which was all he could squeeze in that day. But he left with a big smile and thanks.

When Betty Ford got an invitation to go to the Sans Souci restaurant for lunch, she astounded the city by go-

Ford puts on his jacket in his small dressing room. The door behind him leads to the Fords' bedroom. To the left of the photographer's position is the President's study; to the right, the main hall of the private quarters.

123

ing. With two Secret Service agents (one a woman) seated casually at the adjoining table, she chatted about a hundred things that were now making up her life. She had liked the fact that her youngest son, Steve, who had gone off to be a cowboy for a year rather than attend Duke University, had left with a promise to the staff. "I'll see you soon," he had said, a signal to an anxious mother that at least he wasn't running away. Mrs. Ford told how she wanted to redecorate the Oval Office, revealed that she considered Nelson Rockefeller an excellent dancer and declared her pride in seeing her handsome middle son, Jack, on television dressed in his Yellowstone Park ranger outfit. It was the talk of a wife and mother who just happened to live in the White House. Different—but still not that different.

That human beings were inhabiting 1600 Pennsylvania Avenue was brought home in another way. On a Thursday morning in late September, Betty Ford stopped by Bethesda Naval Medical Center for a routine checkup. Suddenly her world darkened. There was a nodule in her right breast, and the doctors decided that surgery was necessary to determine if it was malignant or not. There was no hesitation. She agreed that she would have the operation in two days. Her life as wife of a politician was none too easy under the best of circumstances, and her fears of what it would be like to live in the White House had been quietly contained. And now this dreaded news. Obviously it produced deep apprehension, but even that she hid from public view. The day before she entered the hospital, Betty Ford moved through her official functions with poise and good cheer. She and the President went to the banks of the Potomac River to attend a ground-breaking ceremony for the memorial grove of trees dedicated

to Lyndon Johnson. There had been many greetings, much laughter as Lady Bird Johnson turned the first spade of earth. Betty Ford was then whisked to the Shoreham Hotel for an appearance at a luncheon for the Salvation Army. The women of the press noted that she was especially pretty and animated in a chic green dress. That afternoon Mrs. Johnson came by the White House for tea in the Oval Room of the residence. It seemed an especially warm moment between these two women who could share an understanding of the job of being a President's wife. A few minutes later, Mrs. Ford slipped away. Concealed in the dark interior of a White House limousine, she took the thirty-minute drive to the towering hospital in Bethesda, checked in quietly and was shown to the presidential suite on the third floor. Her daughter and her secretary were with her. Son Mike and his wife, Gayle, soon joined them. And the President, who was deep into the economic summit meeting, came along later. "It looks like you're having a party," said the President to his wife. The fears were squeezed out as the family drew even closer together, doing those small things that people who care very much about each other do. Susan had scurried off to another floor to deliver a new-baby present to a neighbor for whom she used to baby-sit. Mrs. Ford issued instructions about things to be done in her absence. Being the wife of the President and a focus of national attention was an extra challenge. But as people looked more closely at the new first lady, so often overshadowed in the traumatic events of 1974, they found a person of special dimension. "I went in with a very positive attitude," she said later. It was not that simple, and most people know it.

At six o'clock the next morning she was up. Beside her bed she found three flower arrangements, all gifts from her husband. She went across the hall to join Nancy Howe, her secretary, and the Reverend Billy Zeoli. Soon the children arrived and

once again it was Betty Ford who did the cheering up. She laughed about her toeless operating-room socks ("This will be a new item for *Women's Wear Daily*"). From the start, as she told it later, she knew. "Even though they said they were going to do a biopsy, I knew really that they would have to remove the breast. They moved very fast with me—I knew in my mind this would probably be the outcome....I made up my mind I was going to handle it. I had so much help from my family, I felt as though I owed it to them. I had to come through with flying colors.... I have so much faith in God—I guess I lean a great deal on that. I figure if it's to be, it will be; if it is not, it won't."

At 7:10 a.m. she was wheeled into the operating room. She was still wearing a smile, kidding with the attendants. She eyed the anesthetist and said, "Well, good night, sweet prince." The surgery was performed by Navy Captain William Fouty, chairman of surgery at the hospital. He was assisted by Dr. J. Richard Thistlethwaite, professor of surgery at George Washington University Hospital. What Betty Ford knew in her heart the doctors soon discovered as a fact. They removed the cancerous breast.

The President, on getting the news, choppered to the hospital through a rainstorm and joined his wife in the recovery room, where she was awake but still groggy. While the physicians assured the President that the operation had gone well, the medical news was less comforting. Traces of cancer had been found in two of the thirty lymph nodes removed in the radical mastectomy and that meant further treatment to battle the spread of the disease.

Whatever doubts Betty Ford had in the following days she smothered. Her humor had not been touched by the surgeon's knife, nor had her sense of duty. She had instructions for her family about what to do around the White House. She progressed from chicken broth and crackers to ordering whatever she wanted. Then she was up in a rocking chair and walking about a bit. On the fourth night she was standing in front of the hospital elevator when the visitors came. She even took a Redskins game ball given to the President and tossed a short right-handed pass, which startled the doctors but gave everybody a good laugh and another measure of admiration for a determined woman.

Every afternoon following her classes, Susan Ford came to the hospital to see her mother and talk over the day's doings and help make plans for a return to normalcy. The three boys kept calling from Utah, Montana and Massachusetts. When a White House diplomatic reception came around, Susan substituted for her mother. She put on a new fifty-dollar chiffon gown and performed beautifully through an arduous evening. "Not bad," she said when it was over, "but I would rather have Mother do it." Friends and wives of members of Congress volunteered to help answer the fifty thousand letters of sympathy and good cheer that poured into the White House. Life in the residence bubbled along on Betty Ford's remarkable spirit.

When she came home it was like a festival. Flowers festooned the living quarters. The staff had pasted some of the thousands of get-well cards together and they hoisted signs of welcome out on the back lawn as they awaited her arrival from the hospital. They had planned to sneak some champagne aboard the helicopter that would lift her over the city so that she and the President could have an airborne toast. Somebody forgot the champagne but nobody much cared in the special joy of the moment. What Elizabeth Bloomer Warren Ford had given her family, the presidency and the nation was heady enough.

The President gets acquainted with his dog, Liberty, the golden retriever that has just been presented to him by his daughter, Susan, and photographer David Kennerly. Weeks before, Susan and Kennerly had talked at dinner with Ford about dogs and they had asked him which breed was his favorite. He told them that he liked the female golden retriever best. With that information, Kennerly began a telephone search to kennels across the nation for just the right animal. The dog had been flown in that afternoon from the Midwest. Kennerly and Susan had gone to the airport and brought her to the White House while Ford was off playing golf. To get her used to the new surroundings, they had played with Liberty on the South Lawn, then brought her up to the living quarters and let her roam for a short time. When they heard the President approaching, they put the dog in the family dining room. Ford suspected something was up but he merely asked for a martini and sat down to relax. "Dad," said Susan, "I've got a surprise." She opened the dining room door and out bounded Liberty. The President of the United States was unabashedly pleased. He beamed. "What's this?" he asked first. "Where did she come from? Where did you get her?"

They told him the story and then Susan asked if the dog could be named Liberty. Okay, said the President. Susan explained that she at first thought they could shorten the name to Lib but that might get all mixed up in Women's Lib, so they would have to stick to the full name.

Kennerly now told the story of the search for Liberty. The people at the kennel wanted to know if the recipient of the dog had a big enough house. Yes, assured Kennerly, the family did have a big house. Was the lawn big enough so the dog could run? Indeed, Kennerly said, the lawn was big enough. Was it a good family? Kennerly told them it was a very good family and they lived on a large fenced-in place with plenty of live-in help. Finally he told them it was for the President. "Did they believe you?" asked Ford. "Not at first," said Kennerly. "But I convinced them—then swore them to secrecy." And that is how Liberty, the golden retriever, got her new address.

Like politicians, dogs do not always do what one wants. Betty Ford has a heart-to-heart talk with Liberty at Camp David while the President and ABC's Harry Reasoner stroll through the woods for the television cameras. Liberty was not welcome in this part of the filming and Mrs. Ford applied all the motions and intonations in which she had been instructed by the trainer who had given Liberty obedience lessons. Liberty was being told to "sit" and "stay" in this picture. She was reasonably responsive—but no more.

The President tries his persuasive powers on Liberty. Having had lunch at his desk while Liberty lolled contentedly at his feet, Ford moved on to other duties, only to find his faithful friend following. He turned, dutifully employed the proper dog trainer's gestures and commands, and achieved about the same success his wife had had at Camp David.

Susan Ford, in a new fifty-dollar red chiffon gown, prepares to substitute for her mother as official White House hostess for the white-tie diplomatic reception. Betty Ford was still in the hospital when this traditional event came along, and the President asked his daughter to take over. She did splendidly. After helping Ford button up his "monkey suit," as he called his tails, she joked around with him as he took a call from Mrs. Ford. Here he tells his wife about having got Liberty as a gift earlier in the evening. "It was a great surprise... a great gift." The President and his daughter had been fully briefed by the protocol experts on what to do during the evening. Susan claimed that she might ask some of the stout diplomats to remove their medals before she danced with them. Far right: In the yellow Oval Room, waiting for the diplomats to assemble below, daughter and father have more fun. Susan was laughing about getting a new dress and being able to send the bill to her father. "I am not going to pay for it if it's too much," said Ford. Too late, said Susan, she'd already signed the check.

Rarely can presidential movement be a simple thing. By the time the necessary aides have been assembled, the Secret Service agents added, family members called and those operating the limousines and airplanes alerted, the contingent is sizable. Far right: The President arrives at Bethesda Naval Hospital, where Mrs. Ford went for her cancer operation. Son Mike and his wife Gayle lead a procession off the Marine helicopter on a rainy, cheerless morning. Right: Ford leaves the hospital surrounded by an entourage of aides and hospital staff who had met the President and will now escort him in the limosines back to the helicopter pad.

In the presidential suite at Bethesda Naval Hospital, the President and Mrs. Ford talk with Dr. William Lukash. The first lady's recuperation from her mastectomy was helped by the attentive Ford family. The President and Susan visited almost every day; the sons called at least once a day for progress reports. Far right: The first couple eat lunch in the dining room of the hospital suite.

Left: Mrs. Ford says a sincere good-by to the staff of the Bethesda Naval Hospital who had attended her during her two-week stay. She was a model patient and the farewells had a special bit of feeling, as shown in this picture.
Below: The President and Mrs. Ford wave to the crowd from the helicopter as it lifts off the hospital pad.

The welcome home by Susan, Liberty the retriever and Janet Ford, the President's sister-in-law. This joyful moment was shared by the White House staff, which had assembled around the south stairs, to the left of this picture. They had prepared signs of welcome and get-well wishes for Mrs. Ford.

The private preserve of Mrs. Ford is on the second floor of the White House in the southwest corner of the residence. Left: She takes a few seconds from answering personal mail to play a bit with Liberty, who had wandered to her side looking for some affection. This picture was taken by Fred Ward in mid-November, when Mrs. Ford's schedule was still restricted after her operation. At her desk in the Fords' bedroom, she was answering the special mail from friends whom she wished to write to personally. Right: Mrs. Ford has moved into her private sitting room, where there is another desk. Nancy Howe, her assistant, leans over the desk. The window at the right looks out over the President's office and the Rose Garden, and sometimes Mrs. Ford thumps the glass and waves to the President below. The other window has a view of the South Lawn, the Washington Monument and the Jefferson Memorial.

Paying up. Sometimes even first ladies have to pay their bills with cash. On this afternoon, just a few days before the President left for his Asian trip, Mrs. Ford was attending to details of the presidential wardrobe. A messenger from a Washington men's store had brought around two neckties for the President's morning coat. Below: Mrs. Ford and Nancy Howe check the ties against the formal clothes the President will wear. The cost of the tie selected was a little over seventeen dollars and

the delivery man was waiting down-stairs. Right: Mrs. Ford counts out the ready cash available. She did not have enough on hand. Even with a couple of bucks from Mrs. Howe they were short. Fred came up with the other two dollars, a non-interest-bearing loan that was duly repaid, and yet another White House crisis passed into history.

Perhaps the least photographed part of the White House, aside from the secret installations, is the first couple's bedroom. Here, Mrs. Ford works at her desk in the bedroom. The beds were brought from their Alexandria, Virginia, home. In the administrations of Kennedy, Johnson and Nixon, this was the first lady's bedroom exclusively. Those Presidents had their own bedroom, through the door in the far corner. That room, now the President's study, is where Ford has his exercise equipment and his favorite chair.

Early in the morning just after breakfast, President Ford ponders one of his first decisions—what tie to wear to the office. The tie rack is on the door of his private closet, which is off the President's study. Right: Ford gets one of barber Milton Pitts' special jobs in the White House's basement barbershop. The President continues to work through the haircut. The jolly Pitts was Nixon's barber too. He also cuts the hair of senior staff members and when Vice-President Nelson Rockefeller dropped by the two men did a double take and then agreed they looked alike. Pitts' haircuts, with a shampoo and styling, cost eight dollars—fifty cents cheaper than Pitts' price outside because at the White House he does not have to pay rent.

Ford readies himself for his long day. Tying his necktie is a kind of final ritual which formalizes his dress, puts him in the Chief Executive frame of mind. When he strides out of his private bathroom, Ford is in presidential gear. He puts on his jacket and packs up his briefcase and heads for the Oval Office.

Some of the former athlete's competitive instincts show through in this photograph of Ford playing tennis on the White House court. Because he no longer can take his daily swims, the President plays hard whenever he gets the chance. It was a Sunday-afternoon game of doubles that brought out the fierce look in this picture.

Left: The President gets his soul into a backhand on the White House tennis court. Many people are unaware that there is a court here because it is so well hidden by planting. The court is only a few yards from the Oval Office on the South Lawn and it stands ready at all times for presidential action. Other staff members can sign up to play when the court is not set aside for the President. Ford wears an elastic support on his weakened right knee. Though left-handed, the President plays tennis with his right hand. Right: Ford returns a ball on the Camp David tennis courts. After David Kennerly, Ford's partner in this particular game, had three double faults in a row, the President looked back over his shoulder and fixed a baleful eye on him. "I thought we came out here for exercise," said Ford. "We're not getting any more than it takes to tie shoelaces." Then Ford admonished Kennerly to do what baseball pitchers used to be told—just put the ball in there, straight, and keep it chest high.

What began as another obedience lesson for Liberty on an October afternoon at Camp David ended in a glorious presidential dunking. Ford was walking the dog near the pool when this sequence began. At first he tried to get Liberty to fetch a stick, but the dog ignored all entreaties. Ford threw the stick into the pool, on the assumption that a retriever would like water. Liberty made no effort to obey the presidential commands. Left: Ford finally decided that by example and a little force, he would get Liberty into the water. He rolled his double-knit trousers above his knees and coaxed Liberty into his arms, then lowered her gently into the water. Liberty was not too fond of the idea despite the fact that the water was heated. She scrambled back out on the side. Then, as the President made more appeals to Liberty to come back into the water, Mrs. Ford saw her opportunity. Planting a booted foot gently but firmly on the President's back, she shoved him into the pool.

Next act in the swimming pool drama, far left, included Nancy Howe and Ron Nessen. Taking delight in the President's immersion, Nessen walked to the edge of the pool and leaned down to talk to him. Mrs. Howe came up behind Nessen, gave a well-directed push. Nessen whirled but lost his balance, almost fell on the President. Nessen sputtered, laughed and climbed back on the pool deck with vengeance in mind.

Left: Mrs. Howe got tossed into the Camp David pool by Nessen with very little ceremony and only minor sympathy from the President, who elected to swim a bit since he was already wet. Center: Once again Ford brought the reluctant Liberty into the water as Mrs. Howe struggled to the side. By this time everybody was having a splendid time, the laughter echoing through the Camp David foliage. Only Naval Aide Stephen Todd and the Navy personnel who tend the first family at the camp were not certain how to respond. Such family fun had rarely if ever been part of their routine. Right: Ford shows Liberty the proper form of the dog paddle. At least on this afternoon, Liberty did not develop the same high pitch of enthusiasm for the water that the President always maintains. She swam competently enough but whenever she got the chance she headed toward the steps with the plain intent of making a quick getaway.

Master surveys his new charge. Ford gives Liberty a reassuring heft and pat after she has paddled around the Camp David pool for a short time. Ford's enthusiasm was still undimmed, but Liberty could manage only this expression of wet resignation.

A sodden but laughing President emerges from the pool. And like magic, a member of the Camp David staff materializes at the President's side with a robe and a towel as Ford takes off his wet clothes. He then showered, put on his red sweat suit and went off to the tennis courts for more action. Nancy Howe borrowed some dry clothes from Mrs. Ford. Ron Nessen was loaned an outfit by one of the Navy men.

Father and daughter show their affection. On many afternoons Susan would come home from school, change into the current teen-age fashion—baggy painter's pants—and go out on the South Lawn for a run with Liberty. Then she would come by the Oval Office, check with Secretary Nell Yates to see if she could go inside for a little chitchat. If reading memos alone, even when he was with members of his staff, Ford was always delighted to see Susan. Not since the Kennedy children used to come around for candy from their father had the Oval Office seen such casual family encounters.

The Ford family is unabashed about expressing affection for one another. **Right:** On the South Lawn, Susan says good-by to her father with a kiss while reporters and photographers watch from the White House drive. During this period in early October, Ford took a trip almost every afternoon. Susan would usually see him off on his journeys. Here she is dressed in her Holton-Arms school uniform and the two stand below the rotor of the President's helicopter. **Far right:** The President and his son Steve embrace in the Oval Office as Steve says good-by before he starts to drive across the country in his yellow jeep on the way to his ranch job in Montana.

Steve Ford says good-by to his mother. He had come back to Washington after his mother was operated on for cancer. Mrs. Ford was waiting for the helicopter that would take her and the President out to Camp David for the weekend. Mother and son are talking in the Diplomatic Reception Room on the ground floor of the White House. Far right: The President relishes a dance with Susan at the diplomatic reception when she served as hostess, taking the place of her mother.

The beginning of a big night in Susan's life. She had just got Liberty from the airport and was plotting how she and photographer David Kennerly would surprise her father. At the same time she was having her hair done in preparation for the diplomatic reception later in the night. The small beauty salon is just off the family dining room, on the second floor of the residence. Below: Susan runs with Liberty on the South Lawn. The dog relished the attention from Susan. On good afternoons she religiously went by the kennel to pick up Liberty for her workout.

The President
and
the Presidency

The epicenter of power. Ford sits behind his polished desk in the Oval Office, talking on the phone, toying with his pipe. Behind him is the presidential flag and to the right is a standard with 307 battle streamers commemorating American military engagements from Ticonderoga to Vietnam. Not even those aides who assemble around Ford's desk every day lose their sense of awe at being in this place.

There is no handbook for being President. And historical precedents, while useful, are not definitive. Historical perspective such as that possessed by Harry Truman, who is one of Gerald Ford's models, comes from a lifetime of reading and thinking, not from the preparation of an inaugural address.

The person who comes to occupy the Oval Office is wholly formed. His degree of honesty is fixed, his compassion runs within established limits, his vision has already expanded to its farthest horizons.

Old Harry Truman himself said it pretty well when talking with author Merle Miller in 1961. "Men don't change," the former President said. "The only thing new in the world is the history you don't know."

What we call growth in the man who occupies the presidency is, in many ways, our own education about his character. There may, of course, be hidden energies that spring alive when a person gets the job; there may be talents that have lain dormant for years, that suddenly are discerned only now as they are called into action. The inner resources of most of our Presidents are little known when they take office.

For almost two hundred years and through thirty-six men we have been extremely fortunate. There has been just one true failure. He is Richard Nixon, the only person forced from office, the only man we know about who deliberately violated his oath of office. There are some who still insist that other Presidents have done the same or worse. But it is highly unlikely that history, with its sophisticated techniques of discovery and its horde of gravediggers, has overlooked such a scoundrel.

It is a bit alarming to consider that in this age of exhaustive communication and constant analysis, Nixon gained massive national acceptance. When he was finally stripped bare, what did we discover? The Nixon of Yorba Linda, of Whittier, of Congress, of the vice-presidency. As President he was given a special luster by the power he possessed and by the expectations of the people, but he was made of the same stuff inside from beginning to inglorious end.

It is the same with the great men. Abraham Lincoln's towering place in history did not appear suddenly, overnight. It was constructed of small acts of humility and faith between him and other individuals, the power of clean, simple thoughts of what is right and the eloquence of brevity to express those deeper meanings. He said what he felt, and meant what he said, and he acted on what he meant.

Some suggest the hand of providence has been on the presidential landscape. The strong men like Andrew Jackson and Lincoln and Franklin Roosevelt arrived in the nick of time. The weak men like James Buchanan and Calvin Coolidge presided when the forces of history were in motion and nothing could change them, or else in times when it did not really matter who was in the White House. Those whose administrations were corrupted—Grant and Harding—were reduced to insignificance by an America bursting with confidence and power. With the West to conquer, or with the nation hard at play in the middle of the booming '20s, who worried about Presidents at all?

I have heard people say that a Lincoln could rescue us today. But how can we be sure? Some television specialists declare that Lincoln's melancholy visage would turn off an electorate. Others say that his strength and courage would show through those creased features and that he would be greater than ever in our time.

Somebody said recently that in our current economic difficulty we need Franklin Roosevelt to dispel fear and put together another of his magical programs of recovery. But I have heard it argued with force that a man in a wheelchair could never get into the White House now, cruel as that may seem. It is a little like demanding physical perfection in the men who fly airplanes. Their ultimate courage and judgment cannot be measured, but prudence insists that every measurable characteristic be as close to perfection as possible.

Who could have predicted that Ulysses Grant, the resolute hero of Fort Donelson and Vicksburg, the Union commander who forged a general staff of talented and trustworthy men, would be a hesitant White House patsy, bilked and deceived by his appointees?

And Warren Gamaliel Harding? The reporters of his day eyed a fellow member of the fourth estate (he was publisher of the Marion *Star*) and found his handsome profile and rich baritone irresistible. Some of them confidently wrote that Harding would be one of the great Presidents. And of course what he turned out to be was an easy mark for those hard-eyed opportunists who swarm around the White House.

No man's time in the presidency fits another. The ground shifts even from beneath those who hold the office. It has never been more true than now as we race on in this tormented world.

I watched with misgivings but with profound sympathy as Lyndon Johnson struggled with himself. He wanted to do what Franklin Roosevelt had done—to build houses, raise crops, educate children, provide pensions for those too old to work.
But those days were gone. The problems of the 1960s were largely those of affluence and not of want. The hundreds of bills that Johnson got through Congress piled up on each other, their meaning obscured in our rich and complicated society. And then came the Vietnam war, a struggle that required a new sense of courage (to stay out), a new view of the world. Johnson applied the old nostrums and poured the precious resources of the nation into a war that could not be won.

Richard Nixon did not perceive the spiritual malaise that Johnson left. Nor did he detect the chaos in the domestic economy. Like his Republican mentors of the 1950s, he thought the country could run itself, and he turned to foreign policy, which he believed to be more important and more rewarding for his political life. His foreign triumphs were undermined by the home-front decline, his political demise brought on by indifference and arrogance concerning the rights of individuals.

And now it is Gerald Ford's time.

He is a man of traceable lineage, and his record is open to read. But it is cast now in the format of the presidency, and the problems he confronts are new to him.

Ford sat before a crackling fire in the Red Room one evening shortly before Christmas. Those with him noted that he looked tired. And he confessed as much. The job, he said, was tougher than he had ever imagined. The problems of leadership of such a vast, diverse and angry society were becoming clear. He wondered along with his guests if America was not possessed of some "self-destructive impulse," which brought ruin to institutions and savaged public officials. Neither Ford nor the other men who had been gathered to talk of the future had any answers. The most reassuring thing was that they talked at all about such metaphysical elements in the American perspective.

The great Presidents have all seen the future in one way or another. Most of them have been men of action or else of calculated forbearance. They have been men of moral courage, high idealism and a basic honesty. They have possessed imagination and intelligence and confidence. These qualities have been mixed in varying amounts. And the men have been there at the right time, happenstances of history, who were given the opportunity to act.

How, finally, Gerald Ford will interact with his times and with the challenges he now faces cannot be calculated, because the full depths of him have not been examined and we see only vaguely how events will take us in the critical months ahead.

He looks the way an American president should look. He is on the tall side and bluntly symmetrical, a handsome man with a kind face. On the morning that he stood before the nation and took the oath of office, his appearance was just about all the nation had to go on. It was reassuring. When he walked with Brezhnev on the far edge of Siberia, or swam with France's Valéry Giscard d'Estaing in Martinique, he was an imposing and altogether satisfying figure.

His basic decency instantly restored trust in the presidency. He was solicitous of his predecessor who had fallen. He was magnanimous to those "enemies" who had been treated shabbily through the previous years. The boy scout law is truly a profile of Ford's known life—he is trustworthy, loyal, helpful, friendly, courteous, kind, obedient, cheerful, thrifty, brave, clean and reverent.

His prayers are genuine. His belief in God is not a mockery. There are no East Room services or evangelistic spectacles with political preachers. Ford wrote unabashedly to the Reverend Billy Zeoli, a Grand Rapids evangelist who has become close to the Fords over the years, that Christ was his savior, "my life is his." And each week Zeoli has sent the President a short prayer in the form of a memorandum ("My Dear God, why don't you just come and sit down in this chair and tell me what to do?").

The tone of the Ford presidency is good, as nearly as it can be defined by traditional American virtues. But there is no easy yardstick for greatness, or even adequacy, in the presidency. Lincoln's spirituality was deep though his formal religion was less

181

Nothing focuses American aspirations and endeavors as much as the presidency. Crowds materialize wherever a President goes, no matter how unimportant the occasion. His bearing can set the mood, his smile bring laughter and his scowl cause worry. Right: Ford returns the warmth of a Greensboro, North Carolina crowd. Far right: The President takes his seat after arriving at the final session of the economic summit meeting held the last of September. It was the culmination of a nationwide effort launched by Ford when he first took office. Regional meetings were held in which hundreds of Americans presented their ideas on how to bring the economy out of the doldrums. The results of those sessions were funneled into the summit meeting. Ford used all the data in making his economic plans.

evident. Grover Cleveland, whom history has rated as an able president, had an illegitimate son—or at least he took the responsibility for having fathered a son out of wedlock. And John Kennedy, the Catholic, who did so much to lift the national spirit, lived by a moral code that in some respects would not pass muster in Ford's Episcopal parish.

Ford's mind is sound. His dedication is total. His courage unquestioned. The doubts about his leadership go to more subtle matters, like his perception of the President's role in this time.

He rightly sees that the imperial presidency of Richard Nixon needed to be dismantled—not the power, but the kingly aura. A President must be accountable to the people. There is about Ford at least a little of Truman, who said, "I tried never to forget who I was and where I'd come from and where I was going back to."

But Ford did not at first grasp the full implication of Truman's famous desk sign: "The Buck Stops Here." The idea that Ford should see the future some time before the people did, and that he should declare it and make the decisions to bring it into being, was not written in the first months of his record. His reluctance to clean out the Nixon people and open his doors to talent from a vast spectrum of society, regardless of politics, indicated that he had not examined or accepted all of the Truman doctrine. "All of it belongs to the people," Truman said about the presidency. "It was only lent to me."

There is little doubt among thoughtful men that the opportunity for greatness is there. The presidency, almost alone among the American institutions, seems the one place where the machinery of power is intact, where attention and thought and action can be focused. The Congress, while rousing itself after years of lethargy and divisiveness, is still not asserting its full power. The press, which was so united on Watergate, has broken again into thousands of individual voices. The so-called establishment, which used to design national policy then lent its talented people to help run the government, has grown indifferent and impotent. Much of the leadership of labor seems to run against the mainstream of American intention. And the campuses, which furnished so much creative thought for the government in the postwar period, have not recovered from the years of exile under Nixon.

To understand his limitations, to use his special strengths to bring America together to face the immense tasks before it, is Gerald Ford's challenge. That he had not yet done so completely was the worry as a bitter and scarifying 1974 came to a close. That he seemed to sense this was the hope for the years ahead.

President Ford's easygoing personal qualities, reflected in his smiling face, are in marked contrast to the ceremonial formality that is imposed on our Presidents. One aspect of this formality is the appearance of the presidential seal on practically every object ever handled by the President. Overleaf: The seal appears like magic in an astounding number of places. A lowly pack of cigarettes becomes a collector's item with the presidential seal on the wrapper. Napkins from Air Force One with the seal grandly displayed are saved and pressed in memory books by those lucky enough to get them. The American eagle perches on glassware and china. And just the words "President's House" engraved on the handle of a spoon make it more eloquent than all the other silver patterns. The beauty and the symbolism of the seal is a designer's delight and it is easily adaptable to almost any size, and so it shows up in the presidential rug as well as on the President's cuff links. That loyal and durable eagle used to look toward the arrows of war in his left claw. It was Franklin Roosevelt who decided that he should gaze instead upon the olive branch of peace in his right claw. In 1945, at the end of World War II, Harry Truman signed the order that brought about the change.

American heritage—a night view of Washington. When Poland's Communist Party Boss Edward Gierek came to the White House in October, the formal state dinner began as usual in the second-floor yellow Oval Room, where the top guests were greeted and given cocktails. Gierek noticed the spectacular scene through the tall windows and said something to Ford about it. "Would you like to see Washington's best view?" asked Ford, throwing open the doors and walking out on the Truman balcony. Everyone followed. Ford, an interpreter and Gierek stand in this picture by one of the huge pillars of the south portico. Beyond is the floodlighted Washington Monument and the dome of the Jefferson Memorial.